PRAISE and WORShip

devotional

Gospel Music Association

Tyndale House Publishers, Inc., Wheaton, Illinois

Visit Tyndale's exciting Web site at www.tyndale.com

Praise and Worship Devotional

Copyright © 2004 by Gospel Music Association. All rights reserved.

Devotions written by Steve Siler

Photograph of man reaching copyright © by Photodisc. All rights reserved.
Row of photographs copyright © by Corbis. All rights reserved.

Designed by Luke Daab
Edited by MaryLynn Layman

Music permissions listed in appendix A.

Library of Congress Cataloging-in-Publication Data

Praise and worship devotional / Gospel Music Association.
    p. cm.
Includes bibliographical references and index.
  ISBN 0-8423-8516-9
    1. Devotional literature, English.   2. Contemporary Christian music—Texts.
I. Gospel Music Association.
BV4801.P73 2004
264′.23—dc22   2003020633

Printed in the United States of America

10 09 08 07 06 05 04
7   6   5   4   3   2   1

Contents

Foreword

"It all begins with a song." I don't know who said that origi-
nally, but in Christian music it's one of those truisms that we
go back to again and again.

Song is an especially appropriate medium for the expression of Christian thought and praise to God. That has always
been the case. The apostle Paul admonished the Colossians to
"teach and admonish one another with all wisdom, and as
you sing psalms, hymns and spiritual songs with gratitude in
your hearts to God" (Colossians 3:16, NIV).

What was true two thousand years ago (and before)
remains true today. However, this generation has taken a
new approach to song in the spirit of Psalm 96:1 (NIV): "Sing
to the Lord a new song; sing to the Lord, all the earth."
Contemporary Christian Music sprang from the youth revival
called the "Jesus Movement" that took place in America in
the early 1970s.

Alongside CCM, as the music style has become known,

came contemporary worship music. It was all about a new generation making "a new song" in the musical language the generation knew—that of popular culture.

Contemporary songs of praise made a deep impact on the church in the late twentieth century that has continued into the twenty-first century—an impact that is visible "in all the earth." I have been amazed as I have worshiped with believers in other parts of the world. We all know the same songs, although we sing them in different languages and within our own cultures.

These are new songs, and they have deep meaning to our generation. Despite their popularity, the songs Steve Siler has written about in this book are relatively new, and you may not know many of them. That's OK. In fact, they are partially the reason he wrote this book. It is our hope that you'll find some treasures that are new to you. You'll find a rich storehouse of inspiration here. Hopefully it will lead you to discover anew the power of song.

The Gospel Music Association has a process in which we honor songs and writers each year. Our members, most of whom are involved in Christian/gospel music in some way, vote each year for songs and songwriters that have made an impact in the previous year. In the past thirty-four years hundreds of songs have been nominated for Dove Awards. Sixty of the most inspiring songs, mostly from the last twenty years, have become the inspiration for this devotional book.

You'll enjoy the insights that Steve has pulled from them, but you'll also enjoy the songs themselves. I invite you to read the lyrics and ponder them. Through them, "may the Word of Christ dwell in you richly."

John W. Styll

President, Gospel Music Association

Acknowledgments

Thank you to God the Creator for sharing his gift of creativity with us and for sending us Jesus to teach us how to love one another.

Thanks to Bonnie Pritchard for walking this road with me and bringing it all together—the best part of this process has been getting to call you a friend; Frank Breeden for being the first one to believe in the idea and to John Styll, Mark Ross, and everyone at GMA; Ron Beers, Tammy Faxel, Karen Watson, Janelle Howard, and all of my friends at Tyndale House for letting me write something without music attached; MaryLynn Layman for her skillful editing; Scott Krippayne for sharing an experienced author's perspective with me; Tony Wood for being a walking Christian music encyclopedia; my family—Meredith, Stephanie, and Henry—for letting me toss one more log on the fire; and to Larry Keene for ten years of inspirational sermons.

Thanks also to Rick Atizer, Murray Alboher, Graci Evans,

Adam Greenman, Michael Johnson, Dwight Liles, John Mandeville, Shawn McSpadden, Doris Sanford, Rich Sperber, and my parents, Russ and Carole Siler.

Last but not least, thank you to all the songwriters and publishing companies represented herein for the work you do to create and promote the songs of faith.

Introduction

From as early as I can remember, music has struck a deep chord within me. Growing up in our home meant enjoying a veritable musical smorgasbord. Whether it was belting out "Have an Egg Roll Mr. Goldstone" with Ethel Merman or folding my arms, squatting, and kicking myself into hysterics with my dad while doing "The Russian Saber Dance," music was always at the center of our entertainment. My mom, who had grown up singing in the church, soon introduced me to songs like "The Lord's Prayer," and I realized that music could be more than just entertainment.

The Beatles got my attention—like they did every other kid born in the mid-fifties; I was hooked in 1964 on "I Wanna Hold Your Hand." Weeks later I had my own guitar, and by the age of ten I was writing songs—really bad songs, but songs nonetheless.

After accepting Christ during the summer of my sixteenth year, I wrote my first CCM song, although I didn't know to call it that at the time. It was entitled "No Greater Love."

When I was eighteen, I decided I wanted to be a song-writer. Now admit it, while a songwriter is the kind of person you love to talk to at a party, most of you are not longing for your daughter to bring one home. Be that as it may, songwriters are actually in pretty good biblical company. After all, David—called a man after God's own heart—was a prolific songwriter, writing seventy-nine of the Psalms.

Now as a Christian songwriter some thirty years later, I have had the profound and humbling honor of seeing some of my songs touch human lives. What's more, I have had the even more humbling and more profound experience of hearing the songs of many great and dedicated songwriters that touch my life with words that I have been unable to express myself.

I have learned that music has a way of softening hearts and reaching people with a message that they might not hear any other way. I have seen lyrics create community by helping people see that they are not alone on the road they are walking. I have seen lyrics resonate for someone searching for a new perspective on an old idea, breathing life and excitement into a moribund faith. I have seen lyrics help people to cry much needed tears or to express the overflow of their joy. In short, I have seen lyrics and music help people give expression to the most heartfelt inner part of themselves.

Each of the songs represented here has either won or been nominated for a Dove Award by the Gospel Music Association. While this does mean that fans and industry professionals alike have weighed in positively on the merits of these songs, this collection is by no means intended to offer up the sixty best Christian songs ever written. That is an entirely subjective exercise. Rather, it is the intent here to offer up sixty songs that open a window on themes and ideas worth exploring in more depth.

There are better and easier ways to make money in the world, even in the music business world, than to write Christian songs. Therefore, you can be sure that since the goal of the songwriters represented here is to honor God and reach people for his kingdom, the words of their songs have been written with prayerful consideration.

Also, by no means are the devotions within these pages offered as the only available reflection upon these lyrics. A well-written lyric has many layers and, depending on the personal life experience of the reader, will speak to each reader in different ways. I encourage you not only to reflect on the lyrics in the devotions you find here but also to see what God might have to say exclusively to you through the lyricist's pen.

Occasionally in these pages you will hear me speak in the first person. These are instances where I think my experiences as a parent, in my work, or from my life's faith journey help shed a particular light on the topic at hand.

It is my hope that you find the contents of this book inspirational and challenging. I hope it makes you think. I hope it makes you feel. But most of all I hope it brings you into the presence of our precious Lord Jesus.

Steve Siler

September 2003

Above All

Written by Lenny LeBlanc and Paul Baloche
Recorded by Michael W. Smith
2002 Dove Inspirational Song of the Year

Above all powers
Above all kings
Above all nature and all created things
Above all wisdom and all the ways of man
You were here before the world began

Above all kingdoms
Above all thrones
Above all wonders the world has ever known
Above all wealth and treasures of the earth
There's no way to measure what You're worth

CHORUS
Crucified
Laid behind a stone
You lived to die
Rejected and alone
X *Like a rose trampled on the ground* X
You took the fall and thought of me
Above all

1

ABOVE ALL
Not Your Normal King

Genghis Khan. Napoléon I. Lenin. Hitler.

The pages of history are filled with men who spent their lives trying to enlarge themselves and expand their power, mercilessly killing millions of innocent people in the process. And to what end? They either grew old and weak or were eventually defeated and died, their conquests and domination feeding their megalomania.

Power can be a dangerous, intoxicating motivator, and it seems everybody wants it. How we choose to use power says a lot about in what and in whom we believe.

And yet the One who had the right to claim power and authority over the *whole world* came to earth as an innocent baby and died helplessly on a cross.

Jesus didn't kill anyone or have anyone killed. He didn't put together a great army and ruthlessly crush neighboring nations. He didn't overtax people until they couldn't feed their families in order to build a great palace for himself. He didn't aggrandize himself with royal robes and jewels. He didn't throw opulent parties, strutting around like a peacock and requiring everyone to bow before his presence. He never subjugated the people in any way.

Instead, he washed his disciples' feet. Jesus shared meals with the outcasts and dregs of society. He healed the blind, the lame, and the sick. He forgave people for their shortcomings and mistakes. He defended and blessed the little children. He taught that "whoever wants to be a leader among you must be your servant," adding that he had not come to be served but to serve, giving his life "as a ransom for many" (Matthew 20:26-28). Not very kingly sounding stuff, you say. No, not if your idea of a king is Henry VIII. Jesus turned the concept of what it meant to be a king on its ear.

Because he was *already* above all, he had no need to behave as if he was. Because he *was* God's gift to humanity, he didn't have to act like it. For those who need evidence that Christ was who he said he was, I can think of no greater argument.

Although you and I will probably never be the leader of an army or a country, we're still involved in situations daily that give us the choice between seeking to control others or to serve them.

As a parent, an employer or supervisor, the head of a church committee, a Little League coach, or the child of an aging parent—there are any number of times in our lives when we will find ourselves in authority over others. How will we use that power? We can choose to use it to nurture and encourage, blessing others with an attitude of gratitude and service. Unfortunately, however, the opposite often happens. Feed the fragile human ego a little power, and it can easily become ravenous. If we're not careful, we will shortly be impressed with our own importance and soon be throwing our weight around, bossing people and using them as a means to our own ends.

A Closer Connection

How do you place others above yourself in your service to Christ? Whom do you have power over? How do you use that power to serve others and honor Christ?

A Challenge and . . .

You know that in this world kings are tyrants, and officials lord it over the people beneath them. But among you it should be quite different. . . . Whoever wants to be first must be the slave of all.   MARK 10:42-44

A Promise

"Don't be frightened, Mary," the angel told her, "for God has decided to bless you! You will become pregnant and have a son, and you are to name him Jesus. . . . And he will reign over Israel forever; his Kingdom will never end!"   LUKE 1:30-33

Adonai

Written by Lorraine Ferro, Stephanie Lewis, and Don Koch
Recorded by Avalon
1999 Dove Inspirational Song of the Year

One single drop of rain
Your salty tear became blue ocean
One tiny grain of sand turning in your hand
A world in motion
You're out beyond the furthest morning star
Close enough to hold me in your arms

CHORUS
Adonai
I lift up my heart and I cry
My Adonai
You are Maker of each moment
Father of my hope and freedom
Oh my Adonai

One timid faithful knock
Resounds upon the Rock of Ages
One trembling heart and soul
Becomes a servant bold and courageous
You call across the mountains and the seas
I answer from the deepest part of me

CHORUS

From age to age You reign in majesty
And today You're making miracles in me

ADONAI

A Passionate Creator

Have you ever been to the redwood forests of northern California? These majestic trees are breathtaking. To stand among them is to stand in a natural cathedral. The glory and magnificence of God's creation leaves one in a total state of awe. These silent sentinels, many of whom have stood witness since the time Christ walked the earth, testify to a God capable of miracles—the same God who created you and me.

That's right. The God who created stars that are so far away you can barely see them with the naked eye is the same God who created you and longs to live in your heart. The same God who created the vastness of the ocean is there to wipe away every single tear you cry. And that same God who is capable of creating miracles in nature like the redwoods is capable of creating miracles in you.

Maybe you don't feel very miraculous. Well you should! After all, the God who made rainbows and sunrises made you, too! That's pretty amazing. What's even more amazing is that the God who is the author of the whole universe could be so caring that he desires a personal relationship with each and every one of us!

But if you're anything like me, there are times when you feel like nothing extraordinary could ever happen through you. You're too inexperienced, too discouraged, too stressed, too young, too old, or just too plain tired. You want to make a difference, but you feel uncomfortable or unqualified. You don't have enough education. You don't have enough confidence. You don't have enough money.

Here's the exciting news! God has *already* given us everything we need for the work he wants us to do! In the Beatitudes passage in Matthew, Jesus says, "God blesses those who realize their need for him, for the Kingdom of Heaven is given to them" (5:3). It's exactly when we're most weak that we're ready to be filled with God's strength. Once that happens we're able to do things we never thought possible, things *beyond* ourselves. It all begins with calling out to our Father, maker of us all.

We don't have a dispassionate creator. We have a God who actively seeks to be in relationship with us and is constantly at work in his creation. We can bring every concern of our heart, no matter how small it might seem, before him in prayer. While often we might feel unworthy because of something we have said or done, we need to remember that God will forgive our sins through Jesus if we only ask him to. We can bring *anything* before him. Even our most shameful mistakes, our most troubling experiences, can be transformed by God into blessings for others and ourselves.

It is, in fact, especially those sins over which we have the most guilt and regret that God wishes to extend his forgiveness to us. In the circumstances where we have suffered the greatest injustice and over which we have the most anger, God longs to heal us. Through the regenerative power of Jesus Christ we can be restored and made new. He is at work to bring reconciliation and peace to all of us—a future where we can be free to live joyfully in the light of the love he has for us.

What a comfort to know that the God who spoke the world into existence is still on the job. What a comfort to know that he would step into history to sacrifice for us and redeem us. What a comfort to know he is alive today, changing and remaking those who put their trust in him through his Son, Jesus.

Let us never stop admiring and praising the works of our Creator. Furthermore, may we always honor him as *our* Creator, committing our lives to his care and our hearts to his renewing grace.

A Closer Connection

What are some areas in your life that you thought could never be made new? Prayerfully place all the unresolved pain of your life into the reconciling hands of Jesus Christ.

A Challenge and . . .

Take my yoke upon you. Let me teach you, because I am humble and gentle, and you will find rest for your souls. For my yoke fits perfectly, and the burden I give you is light.
MATTHEW 11:29-30

A Promise

God made Christ, who never sinned, to be the offering for our sin, so that we could be made right with God through Christ.
2 CORINTHIANS 5:21

as friends, family persons I value who are nearing death, I like to think about these words about a future meeting in Heaven

Another Time, Another Place

Carita, Dianne

Written by Gary Driskell
Recorded by Sandy Patty and Wayne Watson
1991 Dove Song of the Year

I've always heard there is a land
Beyond the mortal dreams of man
Where ev'ry tear will be left behind
But it must be in another time
Oh there'll be an everlasting light
Shining a purest holy white
And ev'ry fear will be erased
But it must be in another place

CHORUS
So I'm waiting for another time and another place
Where all my hopes and dreams will be captured
With one look at Jesus' face
Oh my heart's been burnin'
My soul keeps yearnin'
Sometimes I can't hardly wait
For that sweet sweet someday
When I'll be swept away
To another time and another place

I've grown so tired of earthly things
They promise peace but furnish pain
All of life's sweetest joys combined
Could never match those in another time
Oh and though I've put my trust in Christ
And felt His Spirit move in my life
I know it's truly just a taste
Of His glory in another place

10

ANOTHER TIME, ANOTHER PLACE
What Will Heaven Be Like?

The reality of heaven is sure to be glorious beyond anything we can imagine. This lyric frames many beautiful images of the afterlife and confirms our hope in an eternity filled with the joy and the peace of Christ. But is it possible to focus too much on the afterlife? Can we sometimes be in danger of not being the Christians we are called to be in the here and now when we point too single-mindedly toward our days beyond this earth?

Interestingly enough Christ himself doesn't spend any time at all describing heaven. He doesn't talk about what we'll see there, what we'll hear there, or what we'll feel there. His discussions of heaven seem to be much more focused on motivating us to be servants in the world we live in.

Consider the following statements of Jesus:

In Matthew 5:12 Jesus tells that "a great reward" waits in heaven for those who are persecuted for following Christ. In verse 19 Christ says that anyone "who obeys God's laws and teaches them will be great in the Kingdom of Heaven." In Matthew 6:20-21 Jesus tells us to "store your treasures in heaven," rather than on earth, for "wherever your treasure is, there your heart and your thoughts will also be." Later in Matthew 16:19 Jesus says, "Whatever you lock on earth will be locked in heaven, and whatever you open on earth will be opened in heaven." In Matthew 18:3 he says, "Unless you turn from your sins and become as little children, you will never get into the Kingdom of Heaven." This suggests that Jesus thinks that heaven is an enjoyable place and worth aspiring to attain. However, the connection in all of these statements is Jesus' desire for us to understand the way that we should live on earth. How all of this will ultimately translate to the afterlife remains a mystery for those of us still breathing.

So if Jesus, our Lord and Savior, doesn't describe for us what heaven is, how are we supposed to know? Or perhaps an even better question is, are we supposed to know? Why can't we get a clearer picture of heaven from here on earth? I suspect that if any of us could experience the perfect peace and glory of heaven for even one instant, we wouldn't want to stay here on this troubled globe for another minute, and God knows that. Just as God wouldn't let Moses see his face, "for no one may see me and live" (Exodus 33:20), perhaps God can't allow us to see the face of heaven for the same reason.

As a result, we're kept just enough in the dark to remain committed to the journey God has given us here—knowing that at the journey's end there awaits something that's beyond anything we can imagine.

So is heaven lined with streets paved with gold? Are there really wolves lying down with lambs? What exactly awaits us on the other side of this life?

I think it all comes down to this: Our Lord and Savior Jesus Christ offers us the ultimate promise that everyone who believes in him will have eternal life. For those of us who trust him, that should be enough. If it's something he offers, it will be a reward well worth having. Until that day comes—in another time and another place—let's serve him faithfully with all our days in this time and in this place.

A Closer Connection

What sins have you had difficulty turning away from? What does becoming like a little child mean to you? How could you serve Jesus even more in your life?

A Challenge and . . .

Don't be troubled. You trust God, now trust in me. There are many rooms in my Father's home, and I am going to prepare a place for you. JOHN 14:1-2

A Promise

For we know that when this earthly tent we live in is taken down—when we die and leave these bodies—we will have a home in heaven, an eternal body made for us by God himself and not by human hands. 2 CORINTHIANS 5:1

Awesome God

Written by Rich Mullins
Recorded by Rich Mullins
From the 1990 Dove Nominated Praise and Worship Album of the Year

When He rolls up His sleeves He ain't just puttin' on the Ritz
Our God is an awesome God
There is thunder in His footsteps and lightning in His fists
Our God is an awesome God
And the Lord wasn't jokin' when He kicked 'em out of Eden
It wasn't for no reason
That He shed His blood
His return is very close
And so you better be believin'
That our God is an awesome God

CHORUS
Our God is an awesome God
He reigns from heaven above
With wisdom pow'r and love
Our God is an awesome God

And when the sky was starless in the void of night
Our God is an awesome God
He spoke into the darkness and created the light
Our God is an awesome God
The judgment and wrath He poured out on Sodom
The mercy and grace He gave us at the cross
I hope that we have not too quickly forgotten
That our God is an awesome God

AWESOME GOD
Not That Far down to Earth

Have you noticed how the word *awesome* has been trivialized in our culture?

You're more likely to hear someone say, "Wow! What an awesome cheeseburger!" or, "Man that movie was awesome" than you are to hear the word *awesome* used in reverence.

While Rich Mullins's lyric starts out playfully enough, by the time it gets to the chorus it is making a very serious point. According to *Merriam-Webster's Collegiate Dictionary*, the word *awe* means "an emotion variously combining dread, veneration, and wonder that is inspired by authority or by the sacred or sublime."

The New Merriam-Webster's Thesaurus lists only one synonym for *awe*, and that is *reverence*. It does list some of what it calls "related" words. They are *esteem, regard, respect, veneration, worship, admiration, amazement, wonder*, and *wonderment*.

Looking at these two entries one is struck by a thought. Contemporary Christians do a pretty good job of seeing God with wonder and amazement. Esteem, regard, and even respect are part of our relationship with him. Contemporary praise and worship certainly depends largely on our admiration and veneration of God. So in other words, we seem to be doing pretty well with the relative definitions in terms of the way we view God.

But take another look at the actual definition of *awe: dread, veneration,* and *wonder* that is *inspired by authority* or by the *sacred or sublime*. I'm not so sure we're doing quite as well on these.

In contemporary Christianity we have done a pretty good job of distancing ourselves from the fire-and-brimstone God.

The Old Testament is all right, but it's the New Testament where the identity of our God emerges, and he's a warmer, friendlier, more approachable God than the One who brought all that rain down on poor Noah and turned Lot's wife into a pillar of salt. He isn't busy kicking us out of the Garden of Eden. He's trying to fix it so that we can get back into a relationship with him.

There's one problem with that perception. When we focus too much on only the characteristics of God that we are comfortable with, we diminish who God is. We must be very careful that in emphasizing the wonderful qualities of the Son that we don't disregard some of the attributes of the Father.

Our God is a God of mystery. "'My thoughts are completely different from yours,' says the Lord. 'And my ways are far beyond anything you could imagine'" (Isaiah 55:8).

Our God is a God who commands a healthy respect and should be feared, especially by those who would take him too lightly. "Fear of the Lord is the beginning of knowledge. Only fools despise wisdom and discipline" (Proverbs 1:7).

If we begin by revering and worshiping God and obeying his commands, then that respect and discipline will extend into our daily lives and our interactions at places like school and work. We need to be aware that people are going to make judgments about how seriously we take our God from the behavior they observe. And, by the way, God will too!

It's wonderful to have a close, loving relationship with the Savior who came to us as a gentle baby in a manger. However, we must not forget the Father, the author of that supernatural event and Lord of all creation. Yes, in Christ God came to earth. But in our anxiousness to be comfortable with him, let's not bring him *so* far down to earth that we lose our respect and our awe.

A Closer Connection

Which attributes of God have you *not* considered as you worship him? What adjustments might you make in your spiritual discipline to see a larger picture of God?

A Challenge and . . .

Since we are receiving a kingdom that cannot be destroyed, let us be thankful and please God by worshiping him with holy fear and awe. For our God is a consuming fire. HEBREWS 12:28-29

A Promise

In every nation he accepts those who fear him and do what is right. ACTS 10:35

Be the One

Words and Music by Al Denson, Don Koch, and Dave Clark
Recorded by Al Denson
1992 Dove Nominee for Song of the Year

CHORUS
Will you be the one to answer to His call
And will you stand when those around you fall
Will you be the one to take His light into a darkened world
Tell me will you be the one

In a world full of broken dreams
Where the truth is hard to find
For every promise that is kept
There are many left behind
Tho' it seems that nobody cares
It still matters what you do
'Cause there's a difference you can make
But the choice is up to you

CHORUS

O sometimes it is hard to know
Who is right and what is wrong
And where you are supposed to stand
When the battle lines are drawn
There's a voice that keeps calling out
For someone who's not afraid
To be a beacon in the night
To a world that's lost its way

BE THE ONE
The Out Crowd

Mobs are ugly. Nothing good ever happens in a mob. It was a mob mentality that prevailed the day of Christ's crucifixion. In a mob people stop thinking. They allow the passions and the heat of the moment to override their own judgment. They ride on a wave, and often it's a wave that's headed in a very destructive direction. That's a flow with which you don't want to go.

In fact, the exact opposite direction is usually the most Christian path. But it takes being an individual to walk away from a crowd—to go against what everyone else is doing. It takes an individual who is following Christ, the same Christ who taught us that things are quite often different from what they seem.

As if that were not enough, Jesus takes it even one step *further!* He wants us to stand out from the crowd even when it's *not* an angry mob. In our world even the nicest among us are looking out for number one and want to be in first place! But Jesus says in Matthew 20:16, "Those who are last now will be first then."

In our world countries routinely seek supremacy through military might. On a daily basis corporations treat business like a war in which only the strong survive and the big swallow up the small. But in Matthew 5:5 Jesus says, "God blesses those who are gentle and lowly, for the whole earth will belong to them."

Ordinarily we seek to be important and in control, looked up to and admired for our accomplishments. However Jesus presents a different way to live. He says, "Whoever wants to be a leader among you must be your servant, and whoever wants to be first must be the slave of all" (Mark 10:43-44).

We dream about having lots of money and think about all

the wonderful things we could do for the church if we only had more wealth. After many rich people put in large amounts in the temple collection box, a poor widow dropped in two pennies. Then Jesus said, "I assure you, this poor widow has given more than all the others have given" (Mark 12:43).

All of these Scriptures are examples of a God who surprises us by turning things upside-down. It's all backward from what we would expect. And guess what? If you start thinking like this and doing as Christ would have you do, you're definitely not going to be in line with the mob. You're probably not even going to be in line with conventional "wisdom." Forget being part of the in crowd. You're going to stand out from the crowd!

It isn't easy to be the party pooper, the one who is always going against the grain to take a stand. Sometimes it's going to be scary to speak up for what's right, maybe even dangerous. God never promised us that doing things his way would be easy. He has, however, promised to love and never forsake those who put their trust in him.

Don't go along with the crowd. Be the one who stands up for what's right.

Be the one who stands up for Jesus.

A Closer Connection

How do you give more credence to the words of coworkers and family members than to the words of Jesus? In uncomfortable or challenging situations, when did you go along to get along instead of letting the Scriptures guide your response? How did that make you feel?

A Challenge and . . .

Stand your ground, putting on the sturdy belt of truth and the body armor of God's righteousness. Ephesians 6:14

A Promise

God blesses you who are hated and excluded and mocked and cursed because you are identified with me, the Son of Man.

LUKE 6:22

Because He Lives

Written by Bill and Gloria Gaither
Recorded by Bill Gaither Trio
1974 Dove Song of the Year

God sent His Son
They called Him Jesus
He came to love heal and forgive
He lived and died
To buy my pardon
An empty grave is there
To prove my Savior lives

CHORUS
Because He lives
I can face tomorrow
Because He lives
All fear is gone
Because I know
He holds the future
And life is worth the living
Just because He lives

How sweet to hold
Our newborn baby
And feel the pride
And joy he gives
But greater still
The calm assurance
This child can face uncertain days
Because He lives

BECAUSE HE LIVES
The Reason for Our Joy

It has been said that every new baby is God's way of telling
us that he wants the world to go on. It's true there is almost
nothing that brings as much joy as holding a brand-new
baby. Here's a fresh start at life. Somewhere in the back of
our minds we know that the baby is going to grow up and
have to face all the pressures and problems of the world just
like the rest of us, but basking in the bliss of a new birth
we can put all those concerns on the back burner for a while.
The pure contentment of the child as she sleeps washes over
us like a blanket of peace, reminding us that the gift of life
is good and that there's hope for the future.

But *some*day that child will have to grow up, and the
hope and promise of infancy will turn to the cacophony and
confusion of the teenage years. Then will come the pressures
of college, the stress that is the modern work-a-day world,
and the responsibilities of citizenship and raising a family.
Challenges and disappointments will come. Where will that
child's joy come from then?

Ironically it will come from another baby—the Christ
child, God's own Son.

Perhaps no song captures more succinctly the reason for
our joy than this one does. Jesus Christ lived a life of love,
healing, and forgiveness. With his death on the cross, he
bought our pardon from sin, and his resurrection gives us
assurance that he's Lord of all. When we realize that Christ
holds the future, there's nothing to fear. We have eternal life
and eternal peace through him. The twists and turns of this
world may leave us bowed but not broken. Therefore, we
can remain joyful in all circumstances, remembering the
words of the apostle Paul from Philippians 4:12-13: "I have

learned the secret of living in every situation, whether it is with a full stomach or empty, with plenty or little. For I can do everything with the help of Christ who gives me the strength I need."

Our assurance further comes from knowing that Christ has paid for our sins with the greatest act of love in the history of the world and forgives each of us for all of our transgressions. "He has removed our rebellious acts as far away from us as the east is from the west," says David in Psalm 103:12. Through his healing love we have been made new. Paul says in 2 Corinthians 5:17, "Those who become Christians become new persons. They are not the same anymore, for the old life is gone. A new life has begun!" How can we not be filled with joy at this wonderful news?

Of course, as human beings, we always have the option to choose not to experience the joy that comes from knowing Christ. But at that point, that's exactly what it is—*our* choice. We're the only ones who can accept that gift.

Let's face it, none of us knows what our tomorrows will bring, and we all get scared sometimes. But the ability of an uncertain future to steal our joy has been overcome once and for all in the person of Jesus if we but accept him.

Christ, then, is the reason for our joy. May we see in every newborn baby that joy proclaimed anew. And may we live secure in knowing that nothing and no one on earth can ever take our joy away from us—because he lives!

A Closer Connection

How is the joy of knowing Christ reflected in your life? What kind of difference does it make when you trust him as opposed to giving in to fear? Pray for the calm assurance that comes from trusting Christ completely in all things.

A Challenge and . . .

He died once to defeat sin, and now he lives for the glory of God. So you should consider yourselves dead to sin and able to live for the glory of God through Christ Jesus.   ROMANS 6:10-11

A Promise

I am the living one who died. Look, I am alive forever and ever! And I hold the keys of death and the grave.   REVELATION 1:18

Blessed

Words and Music by Cindy Morgan and Ginny Owens
Recorded by Rachel Lampa
2001 Dove Inspirational Song of the Year

I may never climb a mountain so I can see
the world from there
I may never ride the waves and taste the salty ocean air
Or build a bridge that will last a hundred years
But no matter where the road leads
One thing is always clear

CHORUS
I am blessed
I am blessed
From when I rise up in the morning
'Til I lay my head to rest
I feel You near me
You soothe me when I'm weary
Oh Lord for all the worst and all the best
I am blessed

All along the road less traveled
I have crawled and I have run
I have wandered through the wind and rain
Until I found the sun
The watching eyes ask me why
I walk this narrow way
I will gladly give the reason
For the hope I have today

You've given me joy
You've given me love
You give me strength when I want to give up
You came from heaven
To rescue my soul
And this is the reason I know
I know

BLESSED

How's Your Glass?

Have you ever seen children with caterpillars crawling
across their palms? They are full of joy! Their gleeful appre-
ciation for the simplest experience is instinctual. They
haven't yet learned how to be busy. The fine art of shutting
out the wonder of the world around us is something we're
taught. We also learn how to complain, to see ourselves
as not having everything we deserve. However, as far as
blessings go, most of us have all we deserve and much,
much more.

When we're at a crowded supermarket parking lot and the
handicapped spot is the only close space available, do we get
upset over having to park fifty yards away from the store?
Or do we give thanks for the blessing of being able to walk?

When we sit down to pay the bills, do we feel a spirit of
complaint come over us, wondering why everything has to
cost so much? Or are we grateful to live in a country that
affords us a bounty of services and for the job that provides
the income with which to pay for them?

There's so much to be thankful for that if we started thanking God the first thing in the morning, we couldn't finish before bedtime. As Christians we have been admonished to pray without ceasing. Expressing gratitude alone could make that possible.

Ask my father how he is, and he'll always give you the same answer. "Terrific! I woke up breathing again today!" I know, I know. It sounds corny, but it's true.

We have a choice about the way we'll face each new morning. Awakening with a spirit of gratitude and joyfulness can't help but make a difference in the way a day turns out.

Stop and think. When was the last time you gave thanks to God for any of these "ordinary" miracles that touch your life every day, beginning with the air we breathe? the water we drink? What about the ability to see, to hear, and to speak? What about the beauty of a sunset, the music of a songbird, or the splendor of flowers?

Even a bad turn of events is received differently if we reside continually in the peace of Christ. A friend of mine related a story of a man who loaned his new van to some friends. A phone call came that they had been in an accident. The friends were OK, but the van was totaled. The owner of the van responded to the news by saying, "That's all right. This is no surprise to God." In other words, everything will work out. My friends aren't hurt. It's just a vehicle. God will provide the transportation we need or money to repair the van. It's all about attitude.

Charles Swindoll puts it this way: "Attitude, to me, is more important than the facts. It is more important than the past, than education, than money, than circumstances, than failures, than success, than what other people say and do. It is more important than appearance, giftedness, or skill. It will make or break a company, a church, a home. I am convinced that life is 10% what happens to me and 90% how I react to it. And so it is with you. We are in charge of our attitudes."

There's a great irony inherent in Swindoll's remarks. Most of us like to be in control. Yet in the one area where we truly have the control, we give our power away, letting things outside of us determine how we will feel.

So it's up to us. Will we choose stress or peace? Will we choose to see problems or opportunities? Will we hold grudges or be forgiving? Will our glass be half empty or half full?

As children of God we are blessed. As followers of Jesus let's *choose* to see ourselves that way.

A Closer Connection

What current "problems" in your life could you reframe as "opportunities"? How often during the day do you express your gratitude to God?

A Challenge and . . .

Always be joyful. Keep on praying. No matter what happens, always be thankful, for this is God's will for you who belong to Christ Jesus.   I Thessalonians 5:16-18

A Promise

But let all who take refuge in you rejoice; let them sing joyful praises forever. . . . For you bless the godly, O Lord, surrounding them with your shield of love.   Psalm 5:11-12

Circle of Friends

Words and Music by Douglas Kaine McKelvey and Steve Siler
Recorded by Point of Grace
1998 Dove Nominee for Pop/Recorded Song of the Year

We were made to love and be loved
But the price this world demands
Will cost you far too much
I spent so many lonely years
Just trying to fit in
Now I've found a place in this circle of friends

CHORUS
In a circle of friends we have one Father
In a circle of friends we share this prayer
That every orphaned soul will know
And all will enter in to the shelter of this circle of friends

If you weep I will weep with you
If you sing for joy
The rest of us will lift our voices too
But no matter what you feel inside
There's no need to pretend
That's the way it is in this circle of friends

CHORUS
In a circle of friends we have one Father
In a circle of friends we share this prayer
That we'll gather together no matter how the highway bends
I will not lose this circle of friends

Among the nations tribes and tongues
We have sisters and brothers
And when we meet in heaven
We will recognize each other

With joy so deep and love so sweet
Oh we'll celebrate these friends
And a life that never ends

CHORUS
In a circle of friends we have one Father
In a circle of friends we share this prayer
That it will not be long before
All will enter in to the shelter of this circle of friends

CIRCLE OF FRIENDS
A Kingdom Shape

Christians spend a lot of time talking about God's kingdom. Sometimes we're talking about a place, like heaven, or about God's people here on earth. Other times we speak of the kingdom more in terms of God's Spirit or God's presence.

But how else might we describe God's kingdom? If there were an image of God's kingdom, for example, what would it be? May I submit for your consideration a circle?

Perhaps you've been at a church social event where the evening has ended by everybody joining hands and forming a circle. Why do that? What does the circle symbolize? What response does the circle create?

There are five points worth considering about a circle, especially when it is a circle made up of people.

First, a circle is an unbroken chain. When people form a circle, it's an unbroken chain of humanity, with the warmth of each person flowing into another. There's a wonderful sense of community created by the connectedness.

Second, creating a circle with people allows each individual to face every other member of the group at the same time. It allows each person to see and be seen. It affords the opportunity to look everyone in the group in the eye. No one is anonymous.

Interestingly, in a circle no one is *first* in line. Everyone's status is the same, everyone is equally important. No one is excluded. It's a commonwealth.

Also worth noting is that you can't be alone in a circle. There's togetherness. There's community.

Last, just as in Christ, who is the Alpha and Omega, a circle has no beginning and no end. Everyone is cared for. Everyone is valued. Just as no one is outside of Christ's love, no one is outside the circle.

Sometimes in our Christian walk it can become tempting to become rather isolationist in our approach to our faith. After all, we're busy. We've got our jobs and our families. We've got bills to pay, errands to run, and stuff that needs fixing around the house. If we're going to stay in shape, we need to squeeze in some time for our workout routine. At the end of the day we've got just enough energy to read a few pages in that book we've been meaning to get to or for some vege-out time in front of the TV before we fall exhausted into bed. We're lucky if we have just enough time for our own morning devotions and for attending church once a week. It feels like that's about all we can handle.

But the thing that strikes me as I consider the list of qualities found in the circle is the importance of community that it represents. Over and over throughout Scripture we're called to be in community with one another through service and prayer; to weep with those who weep and rejoice with those who rejoice; to love our neighbor, encourage others, and share generously. Paul says in Romans 12:5, "Since we are all one body in Christ, we belong to each other, and each of us needs all the others."

If our schedule is too busy for a regular prayer group, then we're too busy. If our schedule is too busy for us to have time to be in relationship with our neighbors, then we're too busy. And if the only time we're ever at church is for one hour on Sunday, then we're shortchanging ourselves and others in terms of the kind of Christian community and fellowship to which we are called.

In short, we can't be Christians in a vacuum. We must be in community with others to be living the Christian life as Christ would have us live it. Only then will we truly be a circle of friends, a circle of believers caring for and encouraging one another and bringing about God's kingdom here on earth.

A Closer Connection

How are you reaching out to other members of the body of Christ? What are some ways you could be more intentional about creating opportunities for Christian fellowship outside of the regular church service?

A Challenge and . . .

Make me truly happy by agreeing wholeheartedly with each other, loving one another, and working together with one heart and purpose. PHILIPPIANS 2:2

A Promise

Where two or three gather together because they are mine, I am there among them. MATTHEW 18:20

Dive

Written by Steven Curtis Chapman
Recorded by Steven Curtis Chapman
2002 Dove Pop/Contemporary Recorded Song of the Year

The long awaited rains
Have fallen hard upon the thirsty ground
And carved their way to where
The wild and rushing river can be found
And like the rains
I have been carried here to where the river flows yeah
My heart is racing and my knees are weak
As I walk to the edge
I know there is no turning back
Once my feet have left the ledge
And in the rush I hear a voice
That's telling me it's time to take the leap of faith
So here I go

CHORUS
I'm diving in I'm going deep in over my head I want to be
Caught in the rush lost in the flow in over my head
I want to go
The river's deep the river's wide the river's water is alive
So sink or swim I'm diving in

There is a supernatural power
In this mighty river's flow
It can bring the dead to life
And it can fill an empty soul
And give a heart the only thing
Worth living and worth dying for yeah
But we will never know the awesome power
Of the grace of God
Until we let ourselves get swept away

Into this holy flood
So if you'll take my hand
We'll close our eyes and count to three
And take the leap of faith
Come on let's go

DIVE ✓
Don't Be a Dabbler

Everybody needs a hobby. In these busy times people need something to turn their attention to that is just for fun, just to bring some joy. It doesn't really matter what the hobby. It can be stamp collecting, bird-watching, whittling, playing the harmonica, or learning a new language. What is fun to some people would seem like work to others. The main thing is that it just be something that helps a person to relax, to leave the stresses of the daily grind behind.

While sometimes hobbies wind up turning into full-fledged obsessions or sometimes into second careers, mostly they're just things people dabble in. A jigsaw puzzle might sit on the den table for six months, growing piece by piece, one at a time. A watercolor painting might sit on an easel in the basement untouched for weeks. "Oh, do you paint?" "No, I just dabble in it."

Dabbling is fine for hobbies; in fact, it's healthy. There are some things we're *supposed* to dabble in. The minute we make it more than that it becomes another stress point, something that we've *got* to do. Unfortunately, that "dabble" energy can spill over into other areas of our lives that require a deeper commitment. One such area is faith.

A well-known quote says, "Draw nearer to God, and he'll draw nearer to you."

This is a fundamental truth. What we invest in the most will pay the greatest return. Jesus knew this. That's why he said, "Wherever your treasure is, there your heart and thoughts will also be" (Matthew 6:21).

You may have had someone ask, "What faith do you practice?" This is a good question for all of us. If you practice an hour a day on the piano, you're going to get better at it. If you shoot one hundred free throws a day, your free-throw percentage is going to go up. The same thing is true of faith. If you practice your faith—through prayer, Bible study, fellowship with other Christians, outreach to the community and the world, and regular church attendance—you're going to get better at it. It's about commitment. You can't expect to go to church once or twice a month, pick up your Bible only to dust it, pray just at dinnertime, and expect to grow in a meaningful walk with the Lord.

Faith can't be a paint-by-numbers affair because the picture keeps changing. The events of our lives will challenge and stretch our faith, sometimes almost beyond its limits. Our faith must be constantly growing and constantly changing to remain viable. A static faith is a dying faith, irrelevant and hollow.

We can't swim by putting one toe in the water. Neither can we experience faith from the shore. We must dive in. We can't just get a little wet with God's healing stream. It's an all or nothing affair. There's no such thing as a little salvation. We're either saved or we're not. We either immerse ourselves in the living water, drinking in God's love, hope, and mercy, or we thirst for it.

Once we're in the water, we want to stay in. If we get out of the water, we're going to dry off. That's where the practicing comes in. Hobby energy won't work. We've got to keep swimming in the river of faith day by day, growing in belief. Then when the current of life flows against us, as it will, we'll be able to turn to a faith that will be strong enough to sustain us.

So if you want to dabble, go right ahead. Dabble at checkers. Dabble at basket weaving. Dabble at photography. But when it comes to Jesus, no dabbling! Dive into faith!

A Closer Connection

How do you "practice" your faith in Christ? What about your life would make others say that your relationship with Jesus is your number-one priority?

A Challenge and . . .

Let your roots grow down into him and draw up nourishment from him, so you will grow in faith, strong and vigorous in the truth you were taught. Let your lives overflow with thanksgiving for all he has done.   COLOSSIANS 2:7

A Promise

God sent Jesus to take the punishment for our sins. . . . And he is entirely fair and just in this present time when he declares sinners to be right in his sight because they believe in Jesus.
ROMANS 3:25-26

El Shaddai

Written by Michael Card and John W. Thompson
Recorded by Amy Grant
1983 Dove Song of the Year

CHORUS
El Shaddai El Shaddai
El Elyonna Adonai '
Age to age You're still the same
By the power of the name
El Shaddai El Shaddai
Erkamkana Adonai
We will praise and lift You high
El Shaddai

Through Your love and through the ram
You saved the son of Abraham
Through the power of Your hand
You turned the sea into dry land
To the outcast on her knees
You were the God who really sees
And by Your might You set Your children free

CHORUS

Through the years You made it clear
That the time of Christ was near
Though the people couldn't see
What Messiah ought to be
Though Your word contained the plan
They just could not understand
Your most awesome work was done
Through the frailty of Your Son

EL SHADDAI
Not What You'd Expect

It seems like every best-selling book is made into a movie these days. Usually these movies are highly anticipated. The sky is the limit as the studio spends tremendous sums of money to attract the biggest box office stars and creates the most spectacular special effects. The budgets often soar past the 100-million-dollar mark. Yet, how many times have you heard a person say, "Well, the movie was OK, but it wasn't nearly as good as the book"?

Perhaps what the person who liked the book better than the movie was responding to was that the movie was *different* from the book. There were expectations based on having read the book that were not met. The scenes and descriptions in the book were not delivered as imagined.

That may have been the very reason so many of the people who lived at the time of Christ were unable to recognize Jesus as the Messiah. They had read the Scriptures, and they knew the kind of king they were looking for. After all, *El Shaddai* means "God Almighty." The itinerant rabbi from Galilee did not fit the bill.

In eating with sinners (Matthew 9:10-11) and keeping his miracles out of public view (John 7:1-9), Jesus was not meeting the people's expectations for the behavior of their deliverer.

Sometimes I think we're a little too hard on the folks who missed it back in the first century. Somehow, I suspect that if Jesus were to come back today we might make the same mistake. We're used to *big* happenings in this culture. Everything is an event. It's not the professional football championship game. It's the *Super* Bowl. We like hype and lots of it. We want fireworks and supersonic jet flyovers. We want limousines and red carpet walkways.

Rather than making villains out of those who failed to recognize Jesus for who he was, we would do well to take a good hard look at ourselves. We have a lot in common with the people who didn't accept Jesus when they were looking right at him. We're cynical people. We automatically think that there's something wrong with anything that's too good to be true. Wouldn't Jesus'claims have seemed that way to you? We're hard to please. We have sophisticated, high-tech taste. Unless something comes to us in the right package, we instantly dismiss it as unworthy of our time. Would a homeless man and his scraggly band of twelve devotees have convinced you? And of course, first and foremost, we are sinners, just as those who attended the Crucifixion. We don't like being told we're wrong today anymore than folks did two thousand years ago.

The question then becomes, how do we recognize the Messiah when he's not what we're looking for? I mean, sure we're all going to recognize him if he comes riding on the clouds with chariots of fire and trumpets sounding. But what if he comes as an unkempt, foul-smelling, homeless wanderer? What kind of victory are we looking for? Are we looking for a victory for the disenfranchised and the oppressed? Or are we looking for a victory for the ones who look like us and do things our way?

When it comes to recognizing Jesus as the Messiah, we have the benefit of hindsight. We can sit comfortably in our homes and read about how Christ fulfilled eighteen main prophecies, from his virgin birth in Bethlehem to his resurrection to his sitting down at the right hand of God the Father. But as we look forward to the Messiah's return, we need to remember that Christ rarely did the expected, even while he was fulfilling prophecy.

Yes, we serve a God who is almighty and can do grandiose

things. But we don't want to ever become complacent, figuring that we know when and *how* God will act. Let's be vigilant, looking expectantly for Christ in unexpected places.

A Closer Connection
Where do you expect to see Christ? What are some ways you could be more intentional about broadening your expectations?

A Challenge and . . .
Jesus told them, "This is what God wants you to do: Believe in the one he has sent."   JOHN 6:29

A Promise
"My thoughts are completely different from yours," says the Lord. "And my ways are far beyond anything you could imagine. For just as the heavens are higher than the earth, so are my ways higher than your ways and my thoughts higher than your thoughts."   ISAIAH 55:8-9

Embrace the Cross

Written by John G. Elliott
Recorded by Steve Green
1991 Dove Nominee for Inspirational Recorded Song of the Year

I am crucified with Christ
Therefore I no longer live
Jesus Christ now lives in me

Embrace the cross
Where Jesus suffered
Though it will cost
All you claim as yours
Your sacrifice will seem small
Beside the treasure eternity can't measure
What Jesus holds in store

Embrace the love
The cross requires
Cling to the One
Whose heart knew ev'ry pain
Receive from Jesus
Fountains of compassion
Only He can fashion
Your heart to move as His

O wondrous cross our desires rest in you
O Lord Jesus make us bolder
To face with courage the shame and disgrace
You bore upon Your shoulder

Embrace the life
That comes from dying
Come trace the steps
The Savior walked for you
An empty tomb

Concludes Golgotha's sorrow
Endure then till tomorrow
Your cross of suffering
Embrace the cross
Embrace the cross
The cross of Jesus

EMBRACE THE CROSS
A Life Transformed

Madonna frequently wears one on a necklace to accessorize her stage costume. Barry Bonds wears a diamond studded one in his ear. They are for sale at almost every jewelry counter in America. Crosses. The symbol of our Lord's greatest sacrifice reduced to a bauble, a fashion statement—bloodless and unthreatening. Most people wear a cross as a way of showing their belief. But by making the cross ornamental, do we run the risk of trivializing it?

In our churches we hang sanitized versions of the cross on walls and behind altars. We depict it in stained glass and mount it on the outside of our buildings. There's no question we have good intentions. After all, the cross is the symbol of our faith. But by making the cross ubiquitous, do we also contribute to it becoming *less* meaningful?

Let's face it: embracing the cross in America can be fairly easy. Most of us are in no danger of incurring physical recrimination for proclaiming allegiance to the cross. We aren't likely to be fired for wearing a cross to work or arrested for displaying one in our home. The church doesn't require that we pass any kind of test showing our knowledge of the Scriptures or demonstrate any moral superiority before we are permitted to exhibit a cross.

So, if embracing the cross doesn't cost us anything, are we not paying a higher price by failing to realize the full depth of what it represents? What do we miss when we don't embrace the cross in the full measure of its gravity?

"Atonement through the Cross of Christ means that God can put me back into perfect oneness with himself through the death of Jesus Christ without a trace of anything coming between us any longer," writes Oswald Chambers. "I then have to build my thinking patiently to bring it into perfect harmony with my Lord. . . . I have to bring 'every thought into captivity to the obedience of Christ'" (2 Corinthians 10:5 [NKJV]).

Making all our thoughts obedient to Christ *is* going to cost us something.

And there's a paradox inherent here. Yes, we're saved by the grace of God, but, as Dietrich Bonhoeffer wrote in *The Cost of Discipleship,* it must not be a "cheap grace." While we can't earn it, it must *change* us.

So what would embracing the cross look like if we let it change us? It might look like service. It might mean that we care more about doing for others than about doing for ourselves. It might mean that people would see in us a life transformed by compassion and love.

It might look like self-sacrifice. It might mean living in smaller houses or driving less expensive cars in order to share more with those in need. It might mean spending less time at the office and more time in the community. It might mean giving up a comfortable life and doing missions work.

It might even look like suffering. It might mean quitting a job because your faith puts you at odds with the objectives of your employer. It might mean being willing to be publicly ridiculed for your beliefs in order to do what you know Christ would have you do.

These are difficult circumstances, and each of us must prayerfully respond to our personal situation.

But this fact remains: Jesus Christ gave all for us on the cross so that we might have a way to God and victory over sin. There's nothing wrong with believers wearing or displaying the cross of Christ. But let's embrace more than just the symbol. Let's embrace the gospel and point with every day and every action of our lives to the One whom the symbol represents.

A Closer Connection

In what ways is the cross trivialized? Have you grown so used to the cross that you take its significance for granted? In what ways does the cross of Christ have more than a symbolic impact on your life?

A Challenge and . . .

Then Jesus said to the disciples, "If any of you wants to be my follower, you must put aside your selfish ambition, shoulder your cross, and follow me. If you try to keep your life for yourself, you will lose it. But if you give up your life for me, you will find true life." MATTHEW 16:24-25

A Promise

You were dead because of your sins and because your sinful nature was not yet cut away. Then God made you alive with Christ. He forgave all our sins. He canceled the record that contained the charges against us. He took it and destroyed it by nailing it to Christ's cross. COLOSSIANS 2:13-14

Every Season

Written by Nichole Nordeman
Recorded by Nichole Nordeman
2002 Dove Nominee for Inspirational Recorded Song of the Year

Every evening sky an invitation
To trace the patterned stars
And early in July a celebration
For freedom that is ours
And I notice You in children's games
In those who watch them from the shade
Every drop of sun is full of fun and wonder
You are summer

And even when the trees have just surrendered
To the harvesttime
Forfeiting their leaves in late September
And sending us inside
Still I notice You when change begins
And I am braced for cold winds
I will offer thanks for what has been and what's to come
You are autumn

And everything in time and under heaven
Finally falls asleep
Wrapped in blankets white all creation
Shivers underneath
And still I notice You when branches crack
And in my breath on frosted glass
Even now in death
You open doors for life to enter
You are winter

And everything that's new has bravely surfaced
Teaching us to breathe
What was frozen through is newly purposed

Turning all things green
So it is with You
And how You make me new
With every season's change
And so it will be
As You are recreating me
Summer autumn winter spring

EVERY SEASON
A Divine Design

As I write this I'm looking out on a cold, steely gray Nashville morning. It's the kind of day when exhaling makes you look like a steam engine. Twenty-eight degrees. Twelve inches of snow have fallen over the last four weeks followed by several inches of rain the past few days. The ground is muddy, and the trees are the color of aircraft carriers. The tulip poplar that grew two feet in a month when I planted it last summer stands as lifeless and forlorn as a broken car antenna in the middle of the backyard.

But in eight weeks the daffodils and the tulips will poke their bright, cheerful heads up through the warming soil. The shocking yellow tendrils of the forsythia will dance like streaks of sunshine in the breeze. A profusion of white and pink dogwood blossoms will burst upon the scene virtually overnight, dressing the town up as if for a spring cotillion. Azaleas will set garden hedges ablaze. And my tulip poplar will bloom with beautiful flowers, sprout leaves as big as a man's hand, and grow two feet in a month.

The seasons are a divine design, God's road map written

across the face of nature. Without them life would seem monochromatic and not nearly so interesting. They are among God's finest gifts to humanity and another example of his loving, merciful kindness to us. In them we are surrounded each and every day by tangible, visible, and fragrant examples of the touchstones of life. Birth and hope, sowing and playing, reaping and reflecting, rest and death, and finally rebirth are all exemplified here.

In her masterful lyrics, Nichole Nordeman has artfully painted these life events with a bittersweet pen. The young will grow old, strength will surrender to age, and all who love will ultimately experience loss. As the writer of Ecclesiastes says so eloquently, "There is a time for everything, a season for every activity under heaven. A time to be born and a time to die. A time to plant and a time to harvest. . . . A time to cry and a time to laugh. A time to grieve and a time to dance" (Ecclesiastes 3:1-2, 4). There's a sense and an order and a beauty to all things that could not exist apart from a caring, intentional Creator. What a great comfort.

There's a perfect economy to the seasons as they serve their integral purposes in equal measure, by contrast each one informing and complementing the other. So it is with the seasons of our lives. Seasons of want and plenty, of change and stasis, of joy and heartache, of preparation and performance that all ebb and flow to create the journey on this river we call life. God will use one season to teach us lessons we will need to learn for another, never abandoning us, always loving us, and always seeking to draw us closer to him.

While we all will eventually reach our final physical season on earth, there's a death that must come before then for us to reach our full potential. We must die to self. In the spiritual realm there can't be rebirth without death. "For when we died with Christ we were set free from the power of sin," says Paul in Romans 6:7. In John 3:3 Jesus said, "I assure you, unless you are born again, you can never see the Kingdom of God."

Every spring we see a dramatic representation of rebirth as the ground, barren all through the winter, displays vibrant new color. But that beauty is just a hint of what is possible in our own hearts when we are reborn in the image and likeness of Christ. So let's rejoice in whatever season we find ourselves. God is the maker of every season on earth and the maker of our final resting place with him, which will be a season of beauty that will never end.

A Closer Connection

What do you think God is teaching you in this season of your life? Take a leisurely walk through a local park, no matter the time of year, giving thanks for the seasons of the earth and the seasons of your life.

A Challenge and . . .

Let every created thing give praise to the Lord, for he issued his command, and they came into being. He established them forever and forever. His orders will never be revoked.
PSALM 148:5-6

A Promise

God has made everything beautiful for its own time. He has planted eternity in the human heart. ECCLESIASTES 3:11

Farther Than Your Grace Can Reach

Words and Music by Connie Harrington and Steve Siler
Recorded by Jonathan Pierce
1999 Dove Nominee for Inspirational Recorded Song of the Year

I lie awake at night and wonder
How You can still put up with me
I know I push You to the limits
Or so it seems
I start each day with good intentions
Then I fail You in a thousand ways
Somehow You keep forgiving me
For the same mistakes

CHORUS
No fault
No wrong
No dark of night
Can hide me from Your eyes
I cannot fall or climb
Farther than Your grace can reach

I know You've heard this prayer I'm praying
Of what I've done and where I've been
I know I don't deserve Your mercy
But once again

CHORUS

God bless us all the weak and weary
Captives of our flesh and blood
Our only freedom is the refuge
Of Your love

50

FARTHER THAN YOUR
GRACE CAN REACH

A Love You Can't Outrun

When a mother holds her newborn for the first time, she is overcome with emotions! Wonder, inexpressible joy, and a little fear! She has a sense of wanting to protect this noisy, squirming bundle from the big, wide world. She loves her brand-new baby boy or girl unreservedly and unconditionally. There's nothing the child has done, other than simply exist, to elicit this response. Junior hasn't had time yet to bring home any straight-A report cards, give a piano recital, or become a doctor or a lawyer. Mom's total approval is a case of unmerited favor. She loves the baby because the baby is *hers*.

That's exactly how God loves his children. He created us and takes joy in us because we are *his*. We can no more run out of the love of God than a newborn can run out of love from his mother.

Later on that baby is going to grow into a young man or woman. Perhaps he or she will win the Nobel Peace Prize or discover the cure for cancer. Perhaps he will become a teacher, or she will become a police officer, or the child will make the parents proud in some other way. Or maybe the young person will be a horrible disappointment. Likely as not, however—if this is a human child we're talking about—there will be ups and downs for the parents, times of great pride and times of terrible anxiety, times of success and times of failure.

But in any event, that mother will never forget holding her precious little newborn baby. Regardless of how high that child may rise or how low he or she may fall, Mom will still love that child because that child is *hers*.

And if that's true of a human mother, how much more true is that of our God? He loves us with an unfailing love. There's nothing we can do in this life, good or bad, to change that. He loves us in our victories and in our defeats. He loves us when we're caring and generous. He loves us when we're spiteful and greedy. He loves us when we're seeking him with our whole heart and when we're totally lost and confused. This is such good news!

He doesn't withhold his love until we have a certain amount of money in our bank account or until we can afford a house in the "right" neighborhood. He doesn't withhold his love until we lose enough weight to fit into a size six. He doesn't even withhold his love because we are struggling with alcohol abuse or because our marriage has failed or because we have a gambling addiction. Like the old song says, his grace is greater than *all* our sins. We can't fall far enough to escape his love and mercy.

We're talking about a God who is passionate about our freedom! A God who is more interested in helping us achieve freedom from sin through a relationship with him than in seeing us rack up a certain number of brownie points to get into heaven. We're talking about a God who would come to earth as a man and die on a cross to break the bondage that holds us, a God who will pursue us to the ends of the earth to have a relationship with us.

Just like that baby we are all his children. We can't fall or climb farther than his grace can reach.

A Closer Connection

What have you done in the past that made you feel like you were outside of God's love? What does "unfailing love" mean to you? How can you be a good steward of the grace God has extended to you?

A Challenge and . . .

So receiving God's promise is not up to us. We can't get it by choosing it or working hard for it. God will show mercy to anyone he chooses. ROMANS 9:16

A Promise

So let us come boldly to the throne of our gracious God. There we will receive his mercy, and we will find grace to help us when we need it. HEBREWS 4:16

For All the World

Written by Bob Farrell and Greg Nelson
Recorded by Sandy Patty
1992 Dove Inspirational Recorded Song of the Year

Never was the world in such a need of peace
And never has contentment been so hard to find
So many men reaching out their hands
Our brothers and sisters in so many lands
If ever kindness was needed
Then it's crying out to us the time is now

CHORUS
I want the peace
I want the love
For all the world
People of joy with children of hope
For all the world
Father of light
I'll be a light that You can shine through
'Cause You are the peace
And You are the hope
For all the world

What's it gonna take before we show some charity
Compassion and mercy the way it's meant to be
Who'll take the time for the ones who truly need
And pray for a nation that's out on the street
What man is greater than his brother
When in Jesus' eyes we're all the same

CHORUS

Learn a song of freedom and teach it to our children
Let the pipes of peace ring out
And pray the grace of God will lead the way

You are the peace and You are the joy
You are the light
And You are the hope for all the world

FOR ALL THE WORLD
A Bigger Light Than Ours

When we were children, we were taught simple songs, many of which we can still sing word for word at the drop of a hat, such as "This Little Light of Mine." While you may have possibly gone years without singing it, it's still in there. If someone asked you to sing it today, you could probably sing it all the way through. Sometimes I think the message of Christ is supposed to be like that—a simple message of love, peace, and hope that we should be able to remember and share at the drop of a hat.

However, we tend to make the message of Christ more complicated. There have been thousands of books and thousands of songs written about it. There have been millions upon millions of sermons preached and Sunday school classes taught about it. In the process the message has been dissected and subdivided so now we have more Christian denominations than you can count on all ten fingers and toes. All so we can be reminded to love God and love our neighbor as ourselves.

Certainly there is a richness that emerges when we study the unfathomable depths of the Word and seek God diligently. Something happens, though, when we try to micromanage our Christianity. We can inadvertently become too focused on ourselves as individuals or on our own church community, failing to see the opportunities to serve that are all around us. That's when we wind up building a new gymnasium for our youth wing, while single mothers in our own community are trying to feed their families on an income level below the poverty line.

It's one thing to let our light shine to make ourselves feel better or to let our light shine with our friends, family, and loved ones. However, if we're going to ask the Father of light to shine through us, we're going to have to take it farther than that. In John 8:12 our Lord Jesus Christ said, "I am the light of the world." The *world*. Not just our heart, not just our house, not just our street, not just our church, and not even just our country. The world.

How do we proclaim Jesus' light beyond the narrow boundaries of our own life and our own congregation? Jesus gives us a compassionate and compelling answer in Matthew 25, telling us to show hospitality to strangers by feeding the hungry, giving a drink to the thirsty, clothing the naked, caring for the sick, and visiting the imprisoned.

If all the Christians in America were truly living in this way—tithing of their income and of themselves as volunteers—the Christian church would be able to make federal assistance programs obsolete. The coffers of Christian relief organizations around the world would be swelled to overflowing, resulting in food and fresh drinking water for the starving, as well as education, health services, and community improvement programs.

Do you think that those who experience the mercy of Christ firsthand would want to know more about him? If we loved our neighbors the way God has loved us, we wouldn't have to spend any resources trying to find people to evangelize. They would run to us!

Of course, some of this is happening already, but is there ever enough mercy? Can there ever be too much compassion?

Christ did come for all the world. It's up to us as believers to make sure that the world knows about Christ. May our light shine so brightly in the service of others through Christ that all whom we touch will know that Jesus came for them, too.

A Closer Connection

When was the last time your light extended to a stranger? How might you use your time and resources to reflect more of Christ's light to the world around you?

A Challenge and . . .

"Now which of these three would you say was a neighbor to the man who was attacked by bandits?" Jesus asked. The man replied, "The one who showed him mercy." Then Jesus said, "Yes, now go and do the same." LUKE 10:36-37

A Promise

God blesses those who are merciful, for they will be shown mercy. MATTHEW 5:7

For Future Generations

Words and Music by Dave Clark, Mark Harris, and Don Koch
Recorded by 4Him
Recorded by the 1994 Dove Group of the Year

The signs are obvious they are everywhere
All that we hear about is the gloom and despair
Too many would be prophets saying
It's the end of it all
'Cause mother earth can't take much more
The hammer's gonna fall
So nature has its needs that's a lesson learned
But it appears to me there are greater concerns
'Cause we can save the planet thinkin' we will somehow survive
But father time is calling us to save somebody's life

CHORUS
So I won't bend and I won't break
I won't water down my faith
I won't compromise in a world of desperation
What has been I cannot change
But for tomorrow and today
I must be a light for future generations

If we could find a way to preserve our faith
So those who follow us see the price that was paid
Then maybe when they question what it's gonna take to survive
They'll find the strength to carry on in what we leave behind

CHORUS

Lookin' in the eyes of the children
Knowing that tomorrow is at stake
When the choice is up to them
Will they have the strength to say

FOR FUTURE GENERATIONS
A Christian Example

Fast food. Faxes. E-mails. Microwaves. Cell phones. Same-day airfreight. This is modern day society. ASAP has lost its meaning. Everything is ASAP. We want it, and we want it *now*. Not only have the lines between *important* and *urgent* been blurred. In our "I can have it right away if I want to" world, even the lines between *important* and *insignificant* have been blurred. Packages that used to take three or four days in the mail are sent overnight. Food that used to take fifteen minutes to cook is zapped in the microwave. We create an illusion of urgency around the most mundane events and then wonder why we're all so stressed-out.

Along with this instantaneous gratification has come an expectation of convenience and disposability with no consideration of the consequences. Meanwhile our landfills are choked to overflowing. We have plastic garbage that will last for five hundred years, and ten seconds after we have thrown it away it's forgotten. This raises a host of environmental questions about our stewardship of the beautiful planet that God has given us. But it raises an even more serious question about the spiritual legacy we'll pass on to our kids. If an attitude of convenience and disposability permeates our thinking, what does that do to our ability to envision the future of our family and our role in creating that future.

In his challenging book *Anchor Man,* Steve Farrar suggests that parents, especially fathers, have a vital role to play in shaping that future according to the Scriptures. "God expects each father to anchor his family for at least one hundred years," he writes citing Deuteronomy 6. *"These are all the commands, laws, and regulations that the Lord your God told me to teach you so you may obey them in the land you are about to enter and occupy, and* <u>*so you and your children and grandchil-*</u><u>*dren might fear the Lord your God as long as you live*</u> (Deuteronomy 6:1-2, NLT, emphasis mine)."

Clearly God is interested in us taking the long-range view. When we inundate our every waking moment with things that must be done immediately, our focus becomes myopic. We allow the daily minutiae to take on inordinate significance, crowding out things like spirituality and time with family.

This isn't just a message for parents. The "faster is better" trap beckons everyone. All of us have multiple roles as children, friends, coworkers, and neighbors. If you're reading this, there's a pretty good chance you're a church member, too. All of these roles present us daily with marvelous opportunities to touch people's lives in a lasting way. After all, it's the love of Christ that endures forever. All of us have a responsibility to share that love and impact lives for the kingdom. Every bit of love we share in his name is love that will live on long after our earthly lives are over, love that will be passed on by those with whom we have shared it. With each act of love in the present, we're setting a tone for the future. We're also setting an *example*.

Like the song says, this is a world of desperation. It's in this desperation that people try to fill the God-shaped hole with all sorts of noise and activity to lend significance to their lives.

As followers of the gospel of Jesus Christ, let's set a different example. Where there's chaos, let's be committed to peace. Where there's busyness, let's be committed to purpose. Where there's worldliness, let's be committed to godliness. Let's be committed in every generation to sharing the love of Christ that is eternal.

A Closer Connection

What kinds of self-discipline might keep your faith from
breaking down under the weight of modern convenience?
Ask a few trusted prayer partners to point out to you any
weaknesses they might see in your Christian walk.

A Challenge and . . .

*You yourself must be an example to them by doing good deeds
of every kind. Let everything you do reflect the integrity and
seriousness of your teaching.*   TITUS 2:7

A Promise

*The love of the Lord remains forever with those who fear him.
His salvation extends to the children's children of those who are
faithful to his covenant, of those who obey his commandments!*
PSALM 103:17-18

For the Sake of the Call

Written by Steven Curtis Chapman
Recorded by Steven Curtis Chapman
From the 1992 Dove Pop/Contemporary Album of the Year

CHORUS
We will abandon it all
For the sake of the call
No other reason at all
But the sake of the call
Wholly devoted to live and to die
For the sake of the call

Nobody stood and applauded them
So they knew from the start this road would not lead to fame
All they really knew for sure was Jesus had called to them
He said come follow Me and they came
With reckless abandon they came

Empty nets lying there at the water's edge
Told a story that few could believe and none could explain
How some crazy fishermen agreed to go where Jesus led
With no thought for what they would gain
For Jesus had called them by name and they answered

CHORUS

Drawn like rivers are drawn to the sea
There's no turning back for the water cannot help but flow
Once we hear the Savior's call we'll follow wherever He leads
Because of the love He has shown
Because He has called us to go we will answer

CHORUS

Not for the sake of a creed or a cause
Not for a dream or a promise
Simply because it is Jesus who calls
And if we believe we'll obey

FOR THE SAKE OF THE CALL

Someone You Can Trust

Vietnam. Watergate. Iran-Contra. Whitewater. Monica-gate.
Enron.

Americans have been given plenty of good reasons in
recent years to be distrustful of people in positions of authority. The abuse of power has become an all too common occur-
rence in our society. Often, we feel as if we can't trust our
leaders to tell the truth or to keep their word. We've even
had prominent televangelists guilty of keeping their viewers
in the dark about who they were in their private lives and
business practices.

Since the tone for any group of people, be it a small
company or a large country, is set from the top down, this
pattern of dishonesty and deception sends the dangerous
message that it's OK to mislead others in order to get what
you want.

The ends justify the means. Look out for number one, and
if you have to hurt some folks along the way, don't worry.
You can always do some fast-talking or some funny account-
ing later.

This pattern of deceit, once begun, is difficult to contain.
If it's OK to lie at work or in a business deal, then why not lie

to your spouse? This is a very slippery slope. Trust is like fine crystal. It's a very beautiful thing, of great value, and once shattered it's extremely difficult to put back together.

When we answer the call to follow Christ, we are placing our trust in Someone who will never disappoint us, never lie to us, and never forsake us. The bitterness and cynicism fueled by disappointment in our political, spiritual, and business leaders need not set the tone for our lives. In the faithfulness of Christ we find a much higher and completely trustworthy authority that eclipses all others. We find a leader who was willing to die for what he believed, who was willing to give his all for those whom he asked to follow him.

In the book *In His Steps,* Charles Sheldon tells the story of a church in a small town that asks members to take the pledge to do only what they believe Jesus would do, not only in their personal lives but in business as well. Immediately many who make the pledge find themselves in positions where following Christ costs them dearly. A newspaper editor loses advertisers and subscriptions when he starts refusing to run "juicy" stories. A young man loses his job when he refuses a shift change that would force him to work every Sunday. A powerful executive resigns a lucrative position and sheds light on his company's violation of state laws. A young woman with a promising future in opera abandons her career path to devote all of her time to singing in an inner-city mission.

But because they trust completely in Jesus, they follow his lead and watch as their community is transformed with more and more people coming to Christ. Before long, the word is spread to surrounding cities, and other churches make the same remarkable pledge.

For most of us it's natural to want to follow the road most traveled—the safe, established route. It's scary to follow the lead of Christ. He may lead you to places you don't want to go. He may call you to situations where you feel unqualified. He may ask you to do things that don't make sense to the world. But where Jesus calls he will make a way. Just when it looks like you've reached the end of the road, he will provide enough pavement for the next mile. Trust in Christ is never misplaced.

Think about it. Jesus is Someone you can trust *all the time*. He is Someone who has already shown that he was willing to die to save you. So search your heart for Christ's call on your life. And when you hear it, trust it. It's the best game of follow the leader you'll ever play.

A Closer Connection

How do you recognize when Jesus is calling you in a new direction? How often do you pray for Christ's leading in your decision making? What kinds of things would you be willing to give up to follow Christ's call? What wouldn't you give up?

A Challenge and . . .

Jesus called out to them, "Come, be my disciples, and I will show you how to fish for people!" And they left their nets at once and went with him.   MATTHEW 4:19-20

A Promise

O Lord Almighty, happy are those who trust in you.   PSALM 84:12

Forever

Written by Chris Tomlin
Recorded by Michael W. Smith
From the 2002 Dove Praise and Worship Album of the Year

Give thanks to the Lord our God and King
His love endures forever
For He is good He is above all things
His love endures forever
Sing praise sing praise

With a mighty hand and an outstretched arm
His love endures forever
For the life that's been reborn
His love endures forever
Sing praise sing praise
Sing praise sing praise

CHORUS
Forever God is faithful
Forever God is strong
Forever God is with us
Forever forever

From the rising to the setting sun
His love endures forever
By the grace of God we will carry on
His love endures forever
Sing praise sing praise
Sing praise sing praise

FOREVER
The Big Picture

I remember my first serious crush back in junior high school. I was fourteen at the time. My girl friend, Robin, and I made all kinds of plans. We would draw little pictures of ourselves both wearing bib overalls along with our kids—I think we were going to have four—also wearing bib overalls. I couldn't imagine spending my life with anyone else. We promised each other our undying love. When she went away for two weeks on a trip with the Girl Scouts, I cried until I had no tears left because I missed her so much. We promised each other that we were going to be together forever and ever.

Well, Robin and I did get married—but not to each other. It isn't that we didn't mean it when we said we were going to be together forever. It's just that neither of us was very good at predicting the future. My friend Jonathan Watkins says his mother used to say, "Make a plan. Make God laugh."

That doesn't mean we should be irresponsible with the way we face the future. Branch Rickey, the man who signed Jackie Robinson to a contract with the Dodgers, thus breaking major league baseball's color barrier said, "Luck is the residue of design." Certainly preparedness counts for something. Getting a good education, studying the Bible regularly, working hard in order to provide for a family—these are all very important things.

But when it comes to actually predicting the future, we're in over our heads. We need to place our total trust in Someone who has a much bigger picture in mind than we do. After all, our human concepts of forever are so limited. Our time here on earth is but a blip on the radar screen of human history, miniscule in God's eternal timetable.

As Christians we worship the God who is the Alpha and the Omega, the God who is in all, through all, and above all; the God who was, and is, and will always be Lord of all. John 1:1-5 says, "In the beginning the Word already existed. He was with God, and he was God. He was in the beginning with God. He created everything there is. Nothing exists that he didn't make. Life itself was in him, and this life gives light to everyone. The light shines through the darkness, and the darkness can never extinguish it."

Hebrews 13:8 says, "Jesus Christ is the same yesterday, today, and forever." This is the kind of forever that existed before the mountains rose up on the earth and will exist when the mountains of earth are no more. This is the kind of forever that stretches beyond human comprehension.

Without our faith we could choose to be disheartened by this, perceiving our brief lives here on earth as insignificant in the overall scheme of things. But as believers in Christ we are encouraged, knowing that the God who made time itself finds each of us significant enough to be worthy of a relationship with him.

What a tremendous comfort there is in knowing that God not only has been on the job and is on the job but that he will continue to be on the job for *all time to come!* This is a God we can trust with our problems. This is a God we can trust with our careers. This is a God we can trust with the future of our families. This is a God we can trust with everything that we hold dear. This is a God we can trust with our eternity. He is *always* going to be there.

Forever he is faithful. Forever.

A Closer Connection

Do you trust God with your future and the future of your children and grandchildren? How does that trust manifest itself in the way you live your life? Pray for the peace of Christ to be upon your family for generations to come.

A Challenge and . . .

With all my heart I will praise you, O Lord my God. I will give glory to your name forever.   PSALM 86:12

A Promise

Give thanks to the Lord, for he is good! His faithful love endures forever.   PSALM 107:1

Friend of a Wounded Heart

Written by Claire Cloninger and Wayne Watson
Recorded by Wayne Watson
1989 Dove Song of the Year

Smile make them think you're happy
Lie and say that things are fine
And hide that empty longing that you feel
Don't ever show it
Just keep your heart concealed

Why are the days so lonely
I wonder where where can a heart go free
And who will dry the tears that no one's seen
There must be someone
To share your silent dreams

Caught like a leaf in the wind
Lookin' for a friend where you can turn
Whisper the words of a prayer
And you'll find Him there
Arms open wide love in His eyes

CHORUS
Jesus He meets you where you are
O Jesus He heals your secret scars
All the love you're longing for is Jesus
The Friend of a wounded heart

70

FRIEND OF A
WOUNDED HEART
Serving Outsiders

How different the Christian experience in contemporary
American culture is compared to that of first-century
believers. What began nearly two thousand years ago as an
outlawed fringe sect, persecuted by the Roman Empire, has
become the predominant religion of the most powerful
country in the world! Contemporary Christianity now
includes several large denominations with powerful infra-
structures designed to manage the affairs of what amount to
nonprofit, multinational corporations. Belonging to one of
these denominations, especially in a country that openly
embraces Christianity, is likely to make one feel a bit privi-
leged—sort of like an insider.

So what's wrong with that? Don't we want Christianity to
spread? Don't we want our leaders to acknowledge their faith
in Christ? Don't we want our churches to be vibrant and
growing? Yes, yes, and yes. However, there is one thing we
must never lose sight of in the process.

Christ's ministry was not about serving insiders. It was
about serving *outsiders*. Christ ate with sinners. He befriended
prostitutes and tax collectors. Christ was found with the
outcast and the downtrodden. He was concerned about the
one who was lost, not the ninety-nine who were found. He
said it was not the healthy who need a doctor but the sick.

Perhaps you have heard the expression "Comfort the
afflicted and afflict the comfortable." When we become too
comfortable with the status quo, we can easily drift into
complacency, which then can all too easily lead to our being
indifferent to the needs of others. But when he walked the
earth, Christ challenged the status quo and championed the

cause of the weak and powerless. Jesus' words in Mark 9:35 tell us that he wants us to help and serve others. "Anyone who wants to be the first must take last place and be the servant of everyone else."

It's a wonderful privilege to live in a predominantly Christian nation where we are free to worship openly in grand churches. However, many of our churches today provide so many amenities for members that attending church may feel like going to a country club. Even if the majority of Christians feel this is the right model for the church, that doesn't necessarily make it so.

Charles Colson puts it this way: "The longer I'm a Christian the more I realize that the vague deity of American civil religion is a heretical rejection of the Christ of Holy Scripture. So don't confuse your loyalties—never assume the will of the majority and the will of God are synonymous. They may be different—and frequently are."

All of us who have experienced a personal relationship with Jesus know the real peace that his closeness brings in our most difficult times. Perhaps everything is going great for you right now. I hope so. Maybe you've enjoyed the peace of Christ for so long that you've come to take it for granted. I hope *not*. But regardless of the current state of our personal lives, as Christians there's one ongoing responsibility we all share—to proclaim by our words and our Christian walk the Jesus who loves each one of us and longs to save us in spite of our deepest, darkest secrets.

The church's greatness should always, first and foremost, come from its desire to use its power to serve the lost and the powerless. When our buildings and our institutions might, however inadvertently, proclaim a cold, establishment Jesus, unconcerned with the hurting people of the world, we must remember that as followers of Christ we've been called to a

72

mission of *outreach*. As Christians may we be the ones to bring hope to the hopeless, light to those in darkness, and healing to the brokenhearted.

A Closer Connection

Think about the congregational activities you are involved in. Which are self-serving? Which are for the benefit of others? Which accomplish both? What are some ways you could do a better job of being a friend to the brokenhearted in your community?

A Challenge and . . .

All praise to the God and Father of our Lord Jesus Christ. He is the source of every mercy and the God who comforts us. He comforts us in all our troubles so that we can comfort others. When others are troubled, we will be able to give them the same comfort God has given us. 2 CORINTHIANS 1:3-4

A Promise

You can be sure that the more we suffer for Christ, the more God will shower us with his comfort through Christ.

2 CORINTHIANS 1:5

God Is in Control

Written by Twila Paris
Recorded by Twila Paris
1995 Dove Song of the Year

This is no time for fear
This is a time for faith and determination
Don't lose the vision here
Carried away by the motion
Hold on to all that you hide in your heart
There is one thing that has always been true
It holds the world together

CHORUS
God is in control
We believe that His children will not be forsaken
God is in control
We will choose to remember and never be shaken
There is no power above or beside Him we know
Oh God is in control
Oh God is in control

History marches on
There is a bottom line drawn across the ages
Culture can make its plan
Oh but the line never changes
No matter how the deception may fly
There is one thing that has always been true
It will be true forever

He has never let you down
Why start to worry now
Why start to worry now
He is still the Lord of all we see
And He is still the loving Father
Watching over you and me

GOD IS IN CONTROL
The Game Is Decided

On January 3, 1993, the Buffalo Bills and the Houston Oilers met in the AFC Wild Card game. By early in the third quarter the Oilers had taken an insurmountable lead of 35–3. They were in complete control of the game, or so it seemed. Oilers quarterback Warren Moon tried to convince his teammates that they needed to stay focused because there was still a lot of the game left to play, but they couldn't help but feel they had such a huge lead that the outcome was already decided. Then everything began to change. The Bills, for whom nothing had gone right all day, suddenly could do no wrong. By the time the game was over, Buffalo had completed what remains the greatest comeback in the history of the National Football League, winning 41–38.

Control. Everybody wants it. Nobody has it. We all try to convince ourselves that we're in control of various aspects of our lives, but that's an illusion.

Let's think about it for a minute. What's the weather like today? Is it sunny outside, or is it snowing? Certainly the weather is going to affect your day. How much control did you have over the forecast? Do you plan on interacting with any other human beings today? All kinds of things have happened to them so far today that will determine the frame of mind they will bring to their encounter with you. How much control will you exert over those events? Are you your own boss? If not, you don't control whether you'll have a job by the end of the week.

"I am my own boss," you say. Great! Are you in control of the economy? If not, your profitability this year is uncertain. Of course you might have more control if you were in charge of setting government policy. Don't forget government policy involves local, state, and federal levels. Where will you place your involvement?

Let's face it. We're not even in control of whether or not we're going to wake up tomorrow. There's only One who is in control, and we're not the one.

Yes, it's a chaotic world. At times it seems like no one could possibly be in control of the crazy things that are going on all around this planet. But that's only if we take the short-range view. If we pull back for a bigger picture, we see a God who has an eternal plan for our salvation and is constantly at work in the world to heal, reconcile, and redeem his people.

Of course there *are* decisions that we have to make every day, and they do affect our lives. But we always have a choice. We can either choose the pressure and tension of taking everything on ourselves, or we can choose the peace that comes as we seek to follow Christ's lead and prayerfully commit all of our plans to the Lord.

It's not that we need to lie down and give up as if our actions don't count. Instead, there's a place for perseverance. No matter the worldly circumstances, we need to persevere to serve God's kingdom and grow in our relationship with him. But for those who place their trust in Jesus Christ, the final outcome of the game *is* already decided.

So we can choose to let our egos run wild. We can choose to let the fact that we're not in control frustrate us and make us crazy, *or* we can choose to be *comforted* by it. If we seriously consider the situation, it doesn't make a whole lot of sense to take on the responsibility and stress of running the world when the One who created it is already on the job. Why not give God what's his anyway and take his peace in return?

God is in control.

A Closer Connection
In your own life when do you wrestle with God for control? What kind of changes do you need to make in your routine to be more aware daily of God's sovereignty?

A Challenge and . . .
Every child of God defeats this evil world by trusting Christ to give the victory. And the ones who win this battle against the world are the ones who believe that Jesus is the Son of God.
1 JOHN 5:4-5

A Promise
I will not fail you or abandon you.   JOSHUA 1:5

God of Wonders

Written by Marc Byrd and Steve Hindalong
Recorded by Mac Powell, Cliff Young, and Danielle Young
From the 2001 Dove Award-Winning Special Events Album of the Year

Lord of heaven and earth
Lord of all creation
Lord of heaven and earth

Lord of all creation
Of water earth and sky
The heavens are Your tabernacle
Glory to the Lord on high

CHORUS
God of wonders beyond our galaxy
You are holy holy
The universe declares Your majesty
You are holy holy
Lord of heaven and earth
Lord of heaven and earth
Lord of heaven and earth

Early in the morning
I will celebrate the light
When I stumble in the darkness
I will call Your name by night

Hallelujah to the Lord of heaven and earth
Hallelujah to the Lord of heaven and earth
Hallelujah to the Lord of heaven and earth

God of wonders beyond our galaxy
You are holy, holy
Precious Lord reveal Your heart to me
Father holy holy
The universe declares Your majesty
You are holy holy

Hallelujah to the Lord of heaven and earth

GOD OF WONDERS
Gifts for His People

My father-in-law was an incredibly talented artist. He saw the world as few of us see it and translated that beauty onto canvas with pictures that have continued to bless people long after he has passed away. There are two phrases of his that come to mind as I consider the lyrics of this wonderful song. The first is "Thank you, Father."

He believed in saying, "Thank you, Father" for *all* experiences, believing that in everything there was something to be learned. When we think of the vastness of the universe, the beauty of this earth, and the promise of heaven—when we think that we've been blessed to be a part of all that God has created—what else is there to say but, "Thank you, Father." Everywhere we turn there are things to be grateful for: the air we breathe, the water we drink, and the ground we walk on, the green of the grass, the blue of the sky, and the rainbow of flowers. Only a God of wonders, a God of supreme love, could create such gifts and share them with his people.

The other word that comes to mind as I think of my father-in-law is the word that he wanted on his grave marker:

Wonderment. If the natural wonders described above weren't enough all by themselves to elicit this response to the gift of life, then what of God's other gifts to us?

Think of gifts like the love of family and good friends, the blessing of community, and the support of the fellowship of a caring church. Gifts like important work to do and opportunities to share our talents as volunteers. Gifts like beautiful music to stir our souls, great literature to expand our knowledge, and all of the other meaningful forms of expression—dance, art, photography, stage, and film. Gifts like delicious food to eat and miraculous doctors and medicines to help heal us.

I'm sure you could think of many of your own sources of wonderment that extend well beyond this list. But the point is this—the source of all of these remarkable gifts is God. The universe truly does declare his majesty.

To live in denial of that is to live ungratefully. Even the most arrogant and faithless among us must acknowledge that human beings create nothing on our own. The very fact of our existence, which we're not responsible for, makes this indisputable. Everything begins with the wonder of life, and I have yet to meet a human being who could even take credit for his next breath, let alone make a credible defense for taking sole credit for the God-given talents placed in his hands.

So the God of wonders is the creator of life and all the things we experience on earth as well as of the celestial heavens and the eternal heaven. And yet even *that* is not the whole story.

This precious Lord, this holy God, is also the author of our hearts and the author of our salvation. He is our home by day and by night. Through Jesus Christ he has given us a living example of his truth and his light walking among us. Through that same Jesus he has given us forgiveness for everything we could ever do to separate ourselves from him. Through that same Jesus he has given us the Holy Spirit to live in our hearts until we join him in the everlasting. What could be more wondrous than that?

Thank you, Father. Hallelujah to the Lord of heaven and earth!

A Closer Connection
Find ten things to thank the Father for *today!* Make a list and keep it where you can refer to it often and make additions when you think of them.

A Challenge and . . .
Help me understand the meaning of your commandments, and I will meditate on your wonderful miracles. PSALM 119:27

A Promise
My help comes from the Lord, who made the heavens and the earth! PSALM 121:2

God Will Make a Way

Written by Don Moen
Recorded by Don Moen
1992 Dove Nominee for Song of the Year

CHORUS
God will make a way
Where there seems to be no way
He works in ways we cannot see
He will make a way for me
He will be my guide
Hold me closely to His side
With love and strength for each new day
He will make a way
He will make a way

By a roadway in the wilderness
He'll lead me
And rivers in the desert
Will I see
Heaven and earth will fade
But His Word will still remain
He will do something new today

GOD WILL MAKE A WAY
Our Faithful Guide

When I first started a nonprofit organization in 2001, I had no idea how to go about fund-raising. I knew there was a need that we could meet, and I believed that the organization was worthy of support, but I was uncertain how to best go about conveying that message to others. There just didn't seem to be any way for me to get the idea off the ground financially.

Then one day my publisher and I had a business meeting on another matter in Chicago. I flew up from Nashville in the morning and was scheduled to take a 5:00 P.M. flight home. Our meeting took less time than we expected, so we called a car to take us back to the airport in hopes of catching an earlier flight home. After we got into the car, the driver asked if we might pick up another person also heading to the airport. Since we weren't even sure we could make an earlier plane, we agreed. When the next passenger got into the car, we exchanged names and pleasantries. I asked him, "What do you do for a living?" Then came his astounding reply. "I help raise funds for nonprofit Christian charities." Not only did that trip to the airport wind up teaching me a lot about nonprofit fund-raising, but I made a new friend who is actively involved in consulting for my organization some two years later.

I don't live in Chicago. My meeting could have lasted the expected length. I could've called a different transportation company. We could've chosen to fly out of a different airport. You see my point. The odds against this event were astronomical. But with God, all things are possible.

You could probably tell stories of your own like this—times when you have been at an impasse where nothing short of a miracle could help you find your way. A time when it seemed like there was no way out of a bad situation, and suddenly a door you didn't even know was there opened. A time when you didn't know where the money was going to come from, but it came. A time when you couldn't find the right words to speak, but when you needed them, they were there.

Without a doubt, God does not operate on our timetable. It seems like he specializes in coming through at the eleventh hour. Sometimes I think that happens so there will be no way for us to take the credit. When there's no way—when it looks like all is lost and *then* it works out—that's when people begin using a word like *miracle* to explain what's happening. That's when people have their faith strengthened and come to see that God is active in their lives rather than aloof and disinterested.

God cares. To show us just how much he cared he came down to earth in the form of a man. He walked among us. He felt what we felt. From that time until forever he wanted us to know that he could *empathize* with us, that he could understand us. He wanted us to know that we could bring every problem, no matter how great or how small, before him in prayer.

Even though we can't see him physically, that doesn't mean he isn't there. Often we can't see how he's working in our lives without the benefit of hindsight. Jesus knew this would be difficult for us. That's why he said, "Blessed are those who haven't seen me and believe anyway" (John 20:29).

I don't know what you're facing today, but God does, and he's there by your side to faithfully guide you. He will not abandon you. He will not forsake you. Even if what you're going through is something more than you think you can bear, even if it's something you feel like you can't live with, God *will* make a way.

A Closer Connection

What are some difficult situations in your life that have made you question God's sovereignty? How might trusting in God change the outcome of those situations?

A Challenge and . . .

Are any among you suffering? They should keep on praying about it. JAMES 5:13

A Promise

I will make a pathway through the wilderness for my people to come home. I will create rivers for them in the desert!
ISAIAH 43:19

The Great Adventure

Written by Steven Curtis Chapman and Geoff Moore
Recorded by Steven Curtis Chapman
1993 Dove Song of the Year

Started out this morning in the usual way
Chasing thoughts inside my head of all I had to do today
Another time around the circle try to make it better
than the last
I opened up the Bible and I read about me
Said I'd been a prisoner and God's grace had set me free
And somewhere between the pages it hit me like
a lightning bolt
I saw a big frontier in front of me and I heard somebody
say let's go

CHORUS
Saddle up your horses
We've got a trail to blaze
Through the wild blue yonder
Of God's amazing grace
Let's follow our leader into the glorious unknown
This is life like no other
This is the great adventure

Come on and get ready for the ride of your life
Gonna leave long-faced religion in a cloud of dust behind
And discover all the new horizons just waiting
to be explored
This is what we were created for

We'll travel over over mountains so high
We'll go through valleys below
Still through it all we'll find that
This is the greatest journey that the human heart
will ever see
The love of God will take us far beyond our wildest dreams
Yeah oh saddle up your horses come on get ready to ride

THE GREAT ADVENTURE

An Active Religion

In America we've become people who live vicariously. On Saturdays and Sundays in the fall we sit by the millions in our easy chairs, exhorting the modern-day gladiators of the gridiron. If we could be roused for even a simple game of two-handed touch football, a few plays later most of us would be back in our easy chairs nursing a pulled muscle.

Our movies have become bigger, noisier, more violent, and more realistic than ever. Often the images are very disturbing. We're on the beach at Normandy, on the battlefield with William Wallace, or in the middle of some intergalactic war of the universe with space ships blowing up and robots terminating one another. We're front and center for gangland slayings, sexual assaults, and all manner of creatively presented mayhem and murder. All the while we're munching on our popcorn and our chocolate mints sitting in comfortable seats complete with custom drink holders.

Then there's reality television. Watch as ordinary people—just like you and me—fight for survival in the jungle, eat live bugs, jump from airplanes, compete for the "love" of a millionaire, vote each other off an island, out of a house, and back into obscurity. This kind of programming adds an element of voyeurism to the vicarious experience. According to *Scientific American,* a 1999 Gallup poll said that 40 percent of adults and 70 percent of teenagers think they watch too much television—and those are just the ones who would admit it!

Is this why God gave us the precious gift of life? To be spectators? To let others decide what we see, hear, think, and feel?

Within our churches have we been reduced to onlookers? Have we made our congregations into audiences? Most church services tend to unfold in a fairly orderly manner with many even providing bulletins that tell us when to sit, when to stand, and when to say this or that. In *Teaching a Stone to Talk,* Annie Dillard says, "It is madness to wear ladies' straw hats and velvet hats to church; we should all be wearing crash helmets. Ushers should issue life preservers and signal flares; they should lash us to our pews. For . . . God may draw us out to where we can never return."

I dare say that most of us have never really considered our religion much of an adventure. But it ought to be. If we're visiting people in prison, it ought to be an adventure. If we're volunteering at a homeless shelter or a teen pregnancy center, it ought to be. If we're teaching people how to read or building a Habitat house or nursing the sick or comforting the grieving, it ought to be. If we're making our religion not a part but the core of our everyday life so that it manifests itself in our words, our actions, and our prayers, then how can it fail to be anything but an adventure?

God has made us to love one another. He has given us gifts and talents. He has given us a beautiful world. And each and every day, if we but listen, we will find opportunities and challenges to share with one another in this grand adventure called life. Listening, of course, requires that we shut out the noise of modern society. It requires that we, as Dr. Dan Moseley says, "resist enculturation." It requires that we sometimes shut off that box that glows hypnotically in the corner of our living room.

But be careful. Once you start listening and responding to God's call and begin to live an active Christian life, you will likely never be comfortable again being a couch potato! That's OK though. It's not as much fun as real life anyway. And it's not nearly as exciting as having the chance to share the love of Christ and literally save lives and save souls.

So let's saddle up our horses and let God take the reins to draw us out to where we can never return. Is this not the stuff adventures are made of?

A Closer Connection

Do you try to keep Christ in his place or do you let him draw you out of yours? What are some ways you can make your faith a more active part of your life?

A Challenge and . . .

I was hungry, and you fed me. I was thirsty, and you gave me a drink. . . . I was naked, and you gave me clothing. I was sick, and you cared for me. I was in prison, and you visited me.
MATTHEW 25:35-36

God is love, and all who live in love live in God, and God lives in them. 1 JOHN 4:16

The Great Divide

Written by Grant Cunningham and Matt Huesmann
Recorded by Point of Grace
1996 Dove Pop/Contemporary Song of the Year

Silence
Trying to fathom the distance
Looking out 'cross the canyon
Carved by my hands
God is gracious
Sin would still separate us
Were it not for the bridge
His grace has made us
His love will carry me

CHORUS
There's a bridge to cross the great divide
A way was made to reach the other side
The mercy of the Father cost His Son His life
His love is deep
His love is wide
There's a cross to bridge the great divide

God is faithful
On my own I'm unable
He found me hopeless alone
And sent a Savior
He's provided a path
And promised to guide us
Safely past all the sin
That would divide us
His love delivers me

CHORUS
The cross that cost my Lord His life
Has given me mine
His love is deep
His love is wide
There's a cross to bridge the great divide

THE GREAT DIVIDE

Engineers of Love

A man-made bridge over the Akashi Strait in Japan spans 6,532 feet—more than a mile! It's one of nine suspension bridges in the world that stretches over 4,000 feet. As of this writing, a bridge is under design in Italy that will connect the island of Sicily with the Italian mainland. When completed, the Messina strait bridge will have taken eight years to build, cost billions of dollars, and be an astounding 10,827 feet in length.

In addition to bridges we have ocean liners, bullet trains, automobiles, and supersonic jets. Yes, it's absolutely amazing what lengths human beings will go to in order to span great physical distances. Ironically, however, it often seems that in personal interaction exactly the opposite is true.

Husbands and wives won't turn off the TV and look across the room to talk with one another. CEOs fail to recognize the humanity of the employees who work in their companies. Elected officials play politics with the people they are supposed to serve, dividing up ethnic groups like pieces on a chessboard. Leaders of various denominations dishonor Christ by wasting time bickering over nonessentials instead of using their time to share the gospel.

Why did God send his Son to earth? We were too busy loving the law instead of one another. We were allowing the rules to take precedence over people. He needed to get our attention. He wanted to teach us that life is about sharing love, forgiveness, compassion, grace, and mercy. These are things you can't do in a vacuum. You can only share these gifts in relationship with others.

God has given us each other to love. When we separate ourselves from one another, we are separating ourselves from God. Conversely, we show God how much we love him by how well we love one another. He wants us to be connected to other people and to him. Look at the lengths he went to in order to bridge the gap that we created, letting his Son die on a cross. If the shortest distance between God and us is the next person we meet, it seems the least we can do is to take that step, share that love.

What are some ways we can do that? We can start by focusing on what we have in common instead of our differences. We can listen to each other in an effort to understand a little better what it's like to walk in the other person's shoes. We can look to open up and create closeness by unselfishly sharing the best we have to give.

We cannot all be great engineers, building bridges that span thousands of feet across the open water. But even better, we can be bridge builders for Christ.

We can build bridges in our homes, with extended family, with coworkers and neighbors. We can build bridges within our church and in our community. We can look for places where there is division and misunderstanding and seek to be peacemakers. We can look for places where there is the darkness of narrow-mindedness and hate and strive to bring the light of Christ's healing and redeeming love.

If it were possible to build a great bridge to reach God, it would be worth all the time, effort, and money in the world to construct it. Thank God that he has made closing that chasm as simple as saying yes to the gift of salvation through his precious Son, Jesus Christ.

A Closer Connection
What can you say to bring people together through the love of Christ when you hear polarizing, prejudicial remarks? How are you building bridges that others can cross to meet the Savior?

A Challenge and . . .
Love your neighbor as yourself.   MATTHEW 19:19

A Promise
Whether we are high above the sky or in the deepest ocean, nothing in all creation will ever be able to separate us from the love of God that is revealed in Christ Jesus our Lord.   ROMANS 8:39

He Is

Written by Jeoffrey Benward and Jeff Silvey
Recorded by Aaron Jeoffrey
1996 Dove Nominee for Inspirational Recorded Song of the Year

In Genesis He's the breath of life
In Exodus the Passover Lamb
In Leviticus He's our high priest
Numbers the fire by night
Deuteronomy He's Moses' voice
In Joshua He is salvation's choice
Judges lawgiver
In Ruth the kinsmen redeemer
First and Second Samuel our trusted prophet
In Kings and Chronicles He's sovereign
Ezra a true and faithful scribe
Nehemiah He's the rebuilder of broken walls and lives
In Esther He is Mordecai's courage
In Job the timeless redeemer
In Psalms He is our morning song
In Proverbs wisdom's cry
Ecclesiastes the time and season
In the Song of Solomon, He is the lover's dream

CHORUS
He is He is He is

In Isaiah He is Prince of Peace
Jeremiah the weeping prophet
Lamentations the cry for Israel
Ezekiel He's the call from sin
In Daniel the stranger in the fire
In Hosea He is forever faithful
In Joel He's the Spirit's power
In Amos the arms that carry us

In Obadiah He's the Lord our Savior
In Jonah He's the great missionary
In Micah the promise of peace
In Nahum He is our strength and our shield
In Habakkuk and Zephaniah He's pleading for revival
In Haggai He restores a lost heritage
In Zechariah our fountain
In Malachi He's the sun of righteousness
Rising with healing in His wings

In Matthew Mark Luke and John He is God man Messiah
In the book of Acts He is the fire from heaven
In Romans He's the grace of God
In Corinthians the power of love
In Galatians He is freedom from the curse of sin
Ephesians our glorious treasure
Philippians the servant's heart
In Colossians He's the Godhead Trinity
Thessalonians our coming King
In Timothy Titus Philemon He's our mediator and our
faithful pastor
In Hebrews the everlasting covenant
In James the One who heals the sick
In First and Second Peter He is our shepherd
In John and in Jude He's the lover coming for His bride
In the Revelation He is King of kings and Lord of lords

He is He is He is
The Prince of Peace the Son of Man the Lamb of God the
Great I Am,
He's the Alpha and Omega our God and our Savior
He is Jesus Christ the Lord
And when time is no more
He is He is

HE IS
Finish the Book

Have you ever read the Bible *all* the way through? Take a survey among your Christian friends and—if they are honest about it—you'd be surprised how many of them have not actually ever succeeded at this task. Oh, maybe they've read all four of the Gospels through, perhaps even more than once. They might have read the Gospels several times in different translations. They've probably read Psalms. After all, the Psalms are very comforting and relatively easy to understand. Most of us have also managed to read Genesis since it has the distinct advantage of being right at the beginning. I had Genesis practically memorized after my several well-intentioned attempts at reading the entire Bible. Usually I got bogged down somewhere in Leviticus or Numbers. Once I made it all the way to Jeremiah before giving out!

A lot of Christians have made it through the whole New Testament but have never been able to read the entire Old Testament. That was certainly the case with me. I read the New Testament through six times before I finally got serious about finishing the whole Old Testament. At long last in the year 2000, after twenty-six years of being a Christian, I finally finished reading the Bible all the way through. This was after I had already been making my living as a Christian songwriter for seven years!

In the remarkable song "He Is," Jeff Silvey and Jeoffrey Benward have accomplished a seemingly impossible feat. They've written a song that lists all sixty-six books of the Bible. Their song is far from being merely listenable, quite a challenge considering the ambitiousness of their goal, it's musically beautiful and very exciting! But not only is the song educational and informative, it's also provocative. In synopsizing each book of the Bible into one sentence that identifies a quality of God's nature, they have made it readily apparent that the Bible—*all* of the Bible—is God's book.

As Christians we lean heavily on the truth of God's Word. However, how can we truly expect to understand it if we don't take the time to read it and study it for ourselves? It's wonderful to have preachers and theologians, and yes, even songwriters, who prayerfully and faithfully seek to distill the meaning of God's Word for us. All of these are valid ways to experience God's Word when experienced *in addition* to the actually reading of the Word itself. But in no way should sermons, devotionals, or songs take the place of committed Bible-reading time in our spiritual life. That's like eating only gravy without ever bothering with the meat.

It's a busy life we lead here in the twenty-first century. We have lots of good excuses to avoid the things we know we should do. As Christians we must never compromise our spiritual life by neglecting prayer time or Bible-reading time. These must be nonnegotiable if our faith is to be vibrant and alive. If we don't feed ourselves on the life-giving Word of the Lord, we will choose other meals. Eventually a diet of those other meals will leave us spiritually malnourished, hungry for deeper truth.

Maybe you've already read the Bible all the way through. If so, good for you! If not, you have an exciting adventure ahead of you, discovering who he is in the pages of his book. Either way, as people who seek to be the living word in the world, let's be people who read God's Word faithfully, thoroughly, and often!

A Closer Connection
What does the amount of time you spend reading the Bible say about your priorities? In what ways do you approach

your time in the Scriptures so as to create opportunities for deeper understanding? If you haven't read God's Word all the way through, then make a commitment to do so starting today!

A Challenge and . . .

Study this Book of the Law continually. Meditate on it day and night so you may be sure to obey all that is written in it. Only then will you succeed. JOSHUA 1:8

A Promise

Every word of God proves true. PROVERBS 30:5

He is
The Prince of Peace
the Son of Man
the Lamb of God
the Great I Am,
He's the Alpha and Omega
our God and our Savior
He is Jesus Christ the Lord
And when time is no more
He is

He Is Exalted

Words and Music by Twila Paris
Recorded by Twila Paris
Paris is a ten-time Dove Award winner, winning vocalist of the year three times

He is exalted the King is exalted on high
I will praise Him
He is exalted forever exalted
And I will praise His name
He is the Lord
Forever His truth shall reign
Heaven and earth
Rejoice in His holy name
He is exalted the King is exalted on high

HE IS EXALTED
The One True Superstar

"We're number one! We're number one!" It's a familiar refrain in America. We chant it at football stadiums all across America. In addition to number one sports teams, we have movies that are number one at the box office, TV shows that are number one in the ratings, even Christian songs that are number one on the charts! We give out awards at a dizzying clip, heaping disproportionate praise on entertainers, athletes, and other public figures. We casually toss around phrases like *Superstar,* exalting what is temporal and those who will ultimately disappoint us or, at the very least, soon be forgotten.

Few people will remember who won the Academy Award for Best Actor in 1957 or who played in the 1971 World Series. As Irving Berlin once said, "Time has a way of taking a prize and whittling it down to its proper size."

There is one prize, however, that has not been whittled down in value over the last two thousand years. It's the prize the apostle Paul talked about in Philippians 3:14: "I strain to reach the end of the race and receive the prize for which God, through Christ Jesus, is calling us up to heaven."

The reason that prize has not lost any of its value even twenty centuries later is because it's a gift given to us by the only One worthy of exaltation: Jesus Christ.

I've heard some people ask why we need to exalt the name of Christ. Why do we need to praise him? Why do we need to lift his name on high? After all, isn't he already above all? Isn't that high enough? Is his ego so fragile that he needs the praise of a world full of sinners to make him feel good about himself?

C. S. Lewis once said, "I don't pray to God to move God. I pray to God so that I will be moved."

With this statement I think that Lewis hit right at the heart of why we need to exalt Christ. We need to exalt him to remind us who we are in relationship to him. We need to exalt him to keep ourselves mindful of whom we aspire to be in Christ. We need to exalt him lest our egos run away with us and we become inflated with our own importance. We need to exalt him, not because of what it does for him, but because of what it does for *us*.

Sometimes we can become careless with our words, using profanity, or gossip, or speaking hatefully about others behind their back. When we do this, we're not in a right relationship with the Lord. That's why Jesus' brother James reminds us that praising and cursing should not come out of the same mouth (see James 3:9-10). We don't want our attitude of praise to be contradicted by double-mindedness. This is hurtful not only to ourselves and to others but to God as well.

If we're to love others as Christ has commanded us, then we need to be looking up at God, choosing a higher standard. At this point it becomes a matter of obedience. We're lifting God on high and praising his name so that it will transform us and change our hearts. Clearly our praises are meant to elevate our character as we seek to glorify God and come into closer relationship to him through worship.

I'm not saying you shouldn't cheer for your favorite sports teams or enjoy the Oscars broadcast. But we should be ever mindful of and careful about whom we shower adulation upon.

There's only One "Superstar" worthy of our true devotion and worship, of our praise and exaltation—only One whose name is above all names both now and forevermore. His name is Jesus.

A Closer Connection

What are some of the ways your life is transformed through a worshipful relationship with the Lord? How do you seek to honor and extol Christ through your words and actions?

A Challenge and . . .

As they reached the place where the road started down from the Mount of Olives, all of his followers began to shout and sing as they walked along, praising God for all the wonderful miracles they had seen. "Bless the King who comes in the name of the Lord! Peace in heaven and glory in highest heaven!" But some of the Pharisees among the crowd said, "Teacher, rebuke your followers for saying things like that!" He replied, "If they kept quiet, the stones along the road would burst into cheers!" LUKE 19:37-40

A Promise

Rather, the Lord's delight is in those who honor him, those who put their hope in his unfailing love. PSALM 147:11

He Walked a Mile

Written by Dan Muckala
Recorded by Clay Crosse
1998 Dove Nominee for Song of the Year

Before the threads of time began
Was preordained a mighty plan
That I should walk with Him alone
The cords of trust unbroken
But fate foresaw my wandering eye
That none could yet restrain
To violate the friendship
I would cause Him so much pain

CHORUS
And every time I close my eyes
I see the nails
I hear the cries
He did not keep Himself away
He was no stranger to my pain
He walked a mile in my shoes
He walked a mile

Feet so dusty cracked with heat
But carried on by love's heartbeat
A man of sorrows filled with grief
Forgiveness was His anthem
No feeble blow from tongue or pen
Could ever sway my love for Him
Across the echoed hills He trod
And reached into my world

HE WALKED A MILE

In the Game

"When I grow up I'm *never* going to say that to my kids!"

How many parents have found themselves eating those words?

The dramatic shift from a child's point of view to the perspective of parenthood makes parental statements formerly thought of as unfair and arbitrary seem like pearls of wisdom or, at the very least, justifiable frustrations worth venting.

Or how about the employee who suddenly finds him or herself promoted to shift manager? The same person who might have been grousing with his coworkers about what a stickler the supervisor was a week earlier may suddenly be in the position of enforcing the same standards and wondering, *When did my friends get to be such lazy slackers?*

It's easy to have lots of opinions about how some people should behave in a given situation when we don't have to deal with their reality.

I'm reminded of how rudely some fans can behave at sporting events, castigating officials from their seats hundreds of feet from the playing field. "You're blind, Ump! That ball was a mile outside," they scream from the safety of the stadium's upper deck or, more inexplicably, from the cozy confines of their living-room recliners. Meanwhile, which one of these fans has ever had to determine whether a darting, curving, rising, or sinking three-inch sphere covering a distance of sixty feet six inches at between eighty and one hundred miles an hour has successfully crossed a hexagonal piece of rubber through the invisible quadrant located somewhere between the knees and chest of a crouching, moving batter and partially obstructed from view by the frame of a squatting catcher? Oh, and don't forget—all the while being yelled at by anywhere from twenty to fifty thousand hostile strangers. Would you want to try it?

No, we are not supposed to judge others. It might make us momentarily feel better about ourselves to look down on someone else from the leather easy chair of judgment when we've never had to walk a mile in his or her shoes. But it's wrong. In Matthew 7:3 Jesus says, "And why worry about a speck in your friend's eye when you have a log in your own?"

Whenever we spend time seeing life from somebody else's perspective, it changes the way we feel about the situation. It creates empathy, compassion, and understanding. We show more patience with others and more concern for their feelings. Conversely, when someone has had similar experiences to ours, we're likely to feel more understood and less isolated in our own trials.

God knows this about us. After all, he made us. That's why he sent Jesus to walk among us. In doing so he removed forever the distance between himself and us. In the person of Christ, God built a bridge to humanity. Our divine Creator showed he cared enough about us to experience life as we experience it—in the flesh. No longer would we wonder if God knew how we felt. Only a truly loving God would go to such extreme lengths to establish a connection with his people.

In Jesus' short life he experienced every difficult emotion common to the human condition, such as anger (see John 2:14-16), betrayal (see Mark 14:44-45), contempt (see Matthew 23:31-36), frustration (see Matthew 17:17), sadness (see John 11:35), and despair (see Matthew 27:46). He even experienced extreme physical pain on the cross. Whenever we experience any of these emotions in our own life, we can turn in prayer to a loving God who knows firsthand what we're going through.

So the next time you are tempted to feel as if nobody understands, remember that God is in the game with you for every play—not just for today but for every day of your life and eternity beyond. And he never misses a call.

A Closer Connection

How would Christ respond to the mother of three running a household after only four hours of sleep? to the elderly driver in the fast lane? to the harried sales clerk with a long line of impatient customers? Try to put yourself in the shoes of the people you meet today, and love them with the love of Christ.

A Challenge and . . .

Stop judging others, and you will not be judged.   MATTHEW 7:1

A Promise

For we are the temple of the living God. As God said: "I will live in them and walk among them. I will be their God, and they will be my people."   2 CORINTHIANS 6:16

A Heart like Mine

Words and Music by Greg Nelson, Loren Balman, Bryan Duncan, Bob Farrell, and Robbie Buchanan
Recorded by Bryan Duncan
1996 Dove Nominee for Inspirational Song of the Year

Of all the hearts in the world
I've only one to give
So insecure a desp'rate pulse
Racing to Your embrace
That You could want me and seek me
Is more than words could ever say
That You would love me and see in me
A pearl of price thrown away
A heart like mine
How could it be worthy
That You'd find a way to redeem this hardened clay
Twisted and broken
O Father God above
The wonder that You love
A heart like mine

Your holy hands hold me still
Shaping my heart anew
Once vacant shell now reclaimed
Offers its praise to You
The One who searched 'til You found me
A wounded lamb who's gone astray
You stopped the world to recover me
O Lamb of God the price You'd pay for
A heart like mine

A HEART LIKE MINE
The Gift God Always Wants

Sometimes my kids are angels. They are well behaved, cour-
teous, and helpful, filling the house with smiles and laughter
and my heart to overflowing with pride and joy. Then there
are times when my kids are disagreeable and exasperating,
getting into trouble for things they know they're not
supposed to do. Sometimes their behavior is so erratic it's
hard to believe they are the same people—charming one
moment and infuriating the next. There's only one thing
that's consistent in this roller-coaster ride called parenthood—my love for them.

Even when their behavior disappoints me I *still* love them.
In fact, that's when they need my love the most. Not the
kind of love that spoils and coddles, but the kind of love that
guides and corrects.

When I look back at my disobedient acts during my
own childhood through the lens of time, I can see that the
constancy of my father's discipline was a great form of love.

109

I knew he loved me not because I *got* everything but because I didn't get away with *anything!* He loved me openly, was fair, and involved. Even when he was at work, I could feel his presence. To me the greatest punishment imaginable was to disappoint him.

All of this takes on a more extraordinary tone when you realize that he was raised without a father in the home for much of his own childhood.

Maybe it's your perspective of having been a parent that sheds light on your relationship with God the Father. Or maybe having been the child of loving parents shapes your understanding. Perhaps, like my dad, you were given a poor example of what it means to be a father in your own home, or maybe you had no example at all. In any event, a perfect example of a father's love can be experienced by all of us. It's a love that can redeem even the most disobedient heart.

I know sometimes it's hard to imagine that God could even find the time to care about you, especially if you feel you've disappointed him. After all, he's got millions of prayers to answer. He's got pressing, worldly matters that need his attention. *Surely,* you may think to yourself, *he couldn't possibly have time to deal with my problems.* But God isn't the Father of just the powerful and important. He's the Father of all creation, and he cares passionately about each and every one of us. Consider the words of Jesus in Matthew 10:29-30: "Not even a sparrow . . . can fall to the ground without your Father knowing it. . . . So don't be afraid, you are more valuable to him than a whole flock of sparrows."

Just as I seek to nurture and direct my children on a godly path for their lives, and as my father directed me, so our heavenly Father seeks to renew the hearts of all his children. He does not give up on a single one of us. It's not a matter of worthiness. We all have sinned and fallen short of the glory of

God and will do it again. That's where grace comes in. It's the grace of a Father who loves his children and wants what's best for them. It's the grace of a Father who is not as interested in seeing that his children get what they deserve as he is in seeing that they get what they *need*. Finally, it's the grace of a loving Father whose own heart's desire is to be in relationship with us, regardless of the condition of our own heart.

As Christians, all of us hope to lead lives that are pleasing to God. But many of us have fallen short more often than we would have liked and may feel like God must be ashamed of us. Whether your heart is warm and full of peace or shattered into a zillion pieces, it's the only one you have to give, and God the Father wants it exactly as it is. Will you give God that gift today?

A Closer Connection

What secrets do you try to keep from God? Are there rooms in your heart you have kept closed to your heavenly Father? Share your whole heart as a gift, opening up completely before God in prayer.

A Challenge and . . .

Our earthly fathers disciplined us for a few years, doing the best they knew how. But God's discipline is always right and good for us because it means we will share in his holiness.
HEBREWS 12:10

A Promise

The Lord is close to the brokenhearted; he rescues those who are crushed in spirit. PSALM 34:18

The Heart of Worship

Written by Matt Redman
Recorded by Matt Redman
From the Dove 2002 Praise and Worship Album of the Year

When the music fades
All is stripped away and I simply come
Longing just to bring something that's of worth
That will bless Your heart
I'll bring You more than a song
For a song in itself is not what You have required
You search much deeper within
Through the ways things appear
You're looking into my heart

CHORUS
I'm coming back to the heart of worship
And it's all about You
All about You Jesus
I'm sorry Lord for the thing I've made it
When it's all about You
All about You Jesus

King of endless worth
No one could express how much You deserve
Though I'm weak and poor
All I have is Yours ev'ry single breath

THE HEART OF WORSHIP
More Than a Song

With church services often beginning with half an hour or more of praise and worship music, the need for new worship music has burgeoned. While this worldwide phenomenon began in the churches themselves, the music industry has taken swift notice, creating thousands of new songs and signing artists to capitalize on the worship-music trend.

In the past several years worship music has exploded as a musical genre. There was no worship music market when the 1990s began, but from the late 1990s on, worship records have been selling hundreds of thousands of albums per month. Thousands of churches across the country have incorporated praise-and-worship-style music into their services. Praise and worship bands, including guitars, bass, and drums, have replaced the church organ as the preferred method of accompaniment. While churches and denominations will always argue over styles of music and their appropriateness or lack thereof for worship, there's no doubt that large numbers of people enjoy this new type of sacred music.

The lyrics of "The Heart of Worship" raise some interesting questions. Who is all this music really for? What is the purpose of worship?

While there are certainly biblical grounds for praise and worship music, they aren't as abundant as one might suspect, particularly if you focus on the New Testament. Jesus was continually pointing people toward God the Father. Christ himself never commands or asks anybody to praise him. The closest he comes is in Matthew 21:14-16. After healing the lame and the blind in the temple, Jesus said that "even the little children in the Temple [were] shouting, 'Praise God for the Son of David.'" When the priests and elders grew indignant, Jesus quoted Psalm 8:2: "Haven't you ever read the Scriptures? For they say, 'You have taught children and infants to give you praise.'"

Perhaps you could say the servant of all was humble. Not too surprising if you think about his ministry. He was always putting others above himself, and he spent the majority of his time teaching others to do the same. "If you love me, obey my commandments," Jesus said in John 14:15. There's no instruction to praise him. In fact, the only other time Jesus spoke of vertically directed praise is with regard to praising the Father and in association with right behavior. "Let your good deeds shine out for all to see, so that everyone will praise your heavenly Father" (Matthew 5:16).

At the Triumphal Entry in Luke 19:38 the people praise Jesus saying, "Bless the King who comes in the name of the Lord!" And that's it—a grand total of three statements regarding Jesus and praise in the Gospels.

The appeal in Hebrews 13:15 to "continually offer our sacrifice of praise to God by proclaiming the glory of his name" is immediately followed by an appeal to share what we have with those in need, very much in Jesus' model of praise through service.

Only once in the New Testament (James 5:13) is praise music mentioned specifically: "Those who have reason to be thankful should continually sing praises to the Lord." Only in Revelation 5:12-13 are we given the example of Christ being specifically singled out for praise when John writes, "The Lamb is worthy."

Why lay all this groundwork? Simply to say this: It's all about *Jesus*. It's all about praising him by striving to live as he lived. It's all about praising him through our kindness to others. It's all about praising him by sharing his love with the world. It's all about praising him by opening up to him through prayer so that we can be transformed. Praise and worship music is fine and good, but it's who we are when the music stops that interests Christ. Jesus already knows that he is the King of kings and Lord of lords, and he loves to hear that we love him. But he loves even more to see the actions of our lives affirm what we believe.

For it's when we bless the hearts of others that we bless the heart of Christ, and *that's* the heart of worship.

A Closer Connection
How does your worship of Christ look apart from music? Which of your actions demonstrate how you are following Jesus' example of humble service to others?

A Challenge and . . .
All those who love me will do what I say.   JOHN 14:23

A Promise
For the Lord delights in his people; he crowns the humble with salvation.   PSALM 149:4

His Strength Is Perfect

Words and Music by Steven Curtis Chapman and Jerry Salley
Recorded by Steven Curtis Chapman
1990 Dove Inspirational Recorded Song of the Year

I can do all things
Through Christ who gives me strength
But sometimes I wonder what He can do through me
No great success to show
No glory on my own
Yet in my weakness He is there to let me know

CHORUS
His strength is perfect when our strength is gone
He'll carry us when we can't carry on
Raised in His power the weak become strong
His strength is perfect
His strength is perfect

We can only know
The power that He holds
When we truly see how deep our weakness goes
His strength in us begins
Where ours comes to an end
He hears our humble cry and proves again

CHORUS

Raised in His power the weak become strong
His strength is perfect
His strength is perfect

HIS STRENGTH IS PERFECT
Something More Beautiful

Have you ever been to Lower Falls in Yellowstone National Park? It's one of the most beautiful sights of the physical world. Water plunges 308 feet over the cliff and down into the canyon below with a thunderous roar. If you stand on the platform nearest to the falls, you can shout at the top of your lungs and still not be heard.

Most of us tend to think of rock as a hard, strong substance. We certainly would prefer a pillow filled with feathers to one filled with stones. However, the beauty of Lower Falls does not come from the strength of the Rocky Mountains, out of which it is carved, but from their weakness. It's in yielding to the relentless pressure and motion of centuries of water that this inspiring and majestic spectacle has been created.

It's interesting to consider that it is through the rock's weakness that this powerful waterfall has emerged. If the rock had been more resistant, nothing worthy of note would exist. It's only through submission to the water that a magnificent and mighty cascade has been revealed.

Sometimes we can behave like a stubborn stone. God sends living water to run over us, to reshape and polish us into something more beautiful. But we want control, and rather than listen to the song of the babbling brook that God wants to make of our hearts, we build a dam, trying to redirect his flow to our liking and drying up our blessings in the process.

We get caught up in the day-to-day worldly struggles of our lives, trying to be strong, forgetting that it's in our weakness that we're strong. We don't realize that it's when we allow our pride and self-sufficiency to be worn down by God, his perfect strength can begin to work in us.

Of course, the process of being remade in the perfect image of Christ takes time. Lower Falls has taken hundreds of thousands of years to become what it is today. And even now it's being remade as the rock continues to yield to the water.

Likewise, we mustn't try to rush God's chisel either. Just as his strength is perfect, so is his timing. We must trust his loving, guiding hand as we seek to achieve our full potential in him. The flower that unfolds the fastest isn't necessarily the most beautiful. Becoming comfortable in this ongoing state of unfolding is the challenge.

This is perfection sought through submission to God's will—beauty through obedience. It's exactly the opposite of pursuing perfection through control, which is what we all too often try to do. We create unrealistic expectations for ourselves, then get stressed out and beat ourselves up when we continually fall short.

We need to realize that it's not by becoming *more* perfect that we find God. In fact, the only way to find peace and perfection at the same time is by looking to the only One who *is* perfect. It's by coming to the end of ourselves: More of him, less of us.

Sometimes it's easier to get to that place when we are broken by some tragic event in our lives. And *yes*, God's perfect strength is there for us in those moments, but we needn't wait until heartbreak or failure strike to seek God's perfect leading. Instead, let's actively seek to make room for God's refining presence in our hearts at all times. Like a rushing waterfall, let's trust in the One whose perfect strength can polish the rock to make a gem out of our lives.

A Closer Connection

Describe a situation in which you finally admitted your weakness and complete dependence on God. What kind of a difference did it make? What are some of your imperfections that you have not yet acknowledged before God?

A Challenge and . . .

Search for the Lord and for his strength, and keep on searching.
PSALM 105:4

A Promise

I am sure that God, who began the good work within you, will continue his work until it is finally finished on that day when Christ Jesus comes back again.   PHILIPPIANS 1:6

Home Free

Written by Wayne Watson
Recorded by Wayne Watson
1992 Dove Pop/Contemporary Recorded Song of the Year

I'm trying hard not to think You unkind
But heavenly Father if You know my heart
Surely You can read my mind
Good people underneath a sea of grief
Some get up and walk away
Some will find ultimate relief

Home free, eventually
At the ultimate healing
We will be home free
Home free oh I've got a feeling
At the ultimate healing
We will be home free

Out in the corridors we pray for life
A mother for her baby a husband for his wife
Oh sometimes the good die young it's sad but true
And while we pray for one more heartbeat
The real comfort is with You
You know pain has little mercy
And suffering's no respecter of age
Of race or position
I know ev'ry prayer gets answered
But the hardest one to pray is slow to come
Oh Lord not mine but Your will be done

HOME FREE
The Gifts of Suffering

Why is there suffering? I've read the works of many great theologians on this topic and have yet to find a completely satisfying answer. One thing I can tell you is that if you're looking for some overriding sense of fairness to apply to this side of heaven, you won't find it. Good people die, while evil people live. Young, innocent babies die, while elderly people whose minds have drifted away sit idly day after day, living on for years. Life *isn't* fair. But then, I don't read anywhere in the Scriptures that God said it would be fair.

Of course, for those of us who are in the midst of terrible suffering or grief I can offer up the reminder that we will all be at rest with the Lord someday. But to tell someone who has just lost an only child that this beloved child is now celebrating in eternity with Christ is at best a platitude and at worst, thoughtless and cruel. Sometimes the only answer is being present. Listening. Allowing the pain to fill the silence unopposed.

However, since silence doesn't work too well in the world of the written word, let me share a few thoughts about the value of suffering.

Suffering draws us closer together. Funerals, for example, are a time of gathering. We gather to remember, sharing stories and memories of the one who has died. We gather to share the sorrow of others and to grieve with them when words seem inadequate. We laugh, we cry, we hug. The togetherness frees us for a moment from the inescapable pain. We are not alone. In this, our suffering is a reminder of our common humanity.

Suffering teaches us compassion. Once you have truly suffered you'll never look at the suffering of others in quite the same way again. You become more "other" centered, wanting to help. You hate to see others going through what you went through because you know how awful it feels. Instead of mere sympathy, there's empathy. Every time we become a little more concerned with the well being of others above ourselves we draw nearer to the mind of Christ.

Paul expresses it this way: "All praise to the God and Father of our Lord Jesus Christ. He is the source of every mercy and the God who comforts us. He comforts us in all our troubles so that we can comfort others" (2 Corinthians 1:3-4).

Suffering teaches us to not take our blessings for granted. Whether it's a loved one, a pet, a home, a full stomach, money in the bank—there's nothing like not having it anymore to make you appreciate it. Once you've lost things that really matter to you, you're likely to be much more grateful for what you have.

Suffering teaches us how to love. I don't mean romantic love. I mean the unreserved kind of love you have for all the important people in your life once you realize through the experience of loss that they will not always be around. It makes us the kind of lovers who tell our loved ones how we feel about them every time we see them. We pay more compliments. We become more generous with our time and pay better attention to people when we're with them.

Because the pain will not be ignored, suffering teaches us how to live *in the moment*. This is a gift we can take with us into the rest of our lives; living each day to the fullest, we become more aware of the blessings God gives us each and every day. The simplest things become more meaningful and appreciated.

It would be great if human beings could learn all these lessons without ever having to experience pain, but we're just not made that way. We need some bad in our lives in order to truly recognize the good for the gift that it is.

Yes, someday we'll be home with Christ. All the pain and vicissitudes of this life will be left behind. In the meantime, we must remember that the Lord we serve is no stranger to suffering. And whatever you may be going through, he needn't be a stranger to you now.

A Closer Connection

What have you learned about God from the suffering you've experienced? How has that suffering made you a better person? Reach out today with the love of Christ to at least one person who is hurting.

A Challenge and . . .

Are any among you suffering? They should keep on praying about it. JAMES 5:13

A Promise

We know that God causes everything to work together for the good of those who love God and are called according to his purpose for them. ROMANS 8:28

How Beautiful

Words and Music by Twila Paris
Recorded by Twila Paris
1992 Dove Nominee for Inspirational Recorded Song of the Year

How beautiful the hands that served
The wine and the bread and the sons of the earth
How beautiful the feet that walked
The long dusty roads and the hill to the cross

CHORUS
How beautiful
How beautiful
How beautiful is the body of Christ

How beautiful the heart that bled
That took all my sin and bore it instead
How beautiful the tender eyes
That choose to forgive and never despise

And as He laid down His life
We offer this sacrifice
That we will live just as He died
Willing to pay the price
Willing to pay the price

How beautiful the radiant bride
Who waits for her Groom with His light in her eyes
How beautiful when humble hearts give
The fruit of pure lives so that others may live

How beautiful the feet that bring
The sound of good news and the love of the King
How beautiful the hands that serve
The wine and the bread and the sons of the earth

HOW BEAUTIFUL
Who Is the Beholder?

Beauty, they say, is in the eye of the beholder. Apparently, however, we human beings are not content to let that be. We want to help the beholders along a little bit. That's why cosmetics are a multi*billion*-dollar industry.

We have become a culture obsessed with appearance. In many cases this extends to Christians as well. Unfortunately, our young girls are getting the message. In her book *Reviving Ophelia*, Dr. Mary Pipher tells haunting tales of girls trying to starve their way to "beauty." These are girls who need to see themselves as being created by a God who loves them unconditionally—who loves them for who they are, not for what they look like.

So how do we change our culture to be a place where our young people feel valued for who they *are*, instead of one where they are emotionally destroyed for not being who they were never intended to be? How do we turn down the pressure on our youth that causes them to despair because they don't look like runway models or their favorite movie stars? The answer—by refocusing on Christ.

We need to take the focus off of external things and put it on things *eternal*. The sweetest frame will bend with age. Physical beauty is as fleeting as the wind. Only the love of God is forever. And that love is the one thing God wants all of us to wear. Paul says in Colossians 3:14, "The most important piece of clothing you must wear is love." This is a message we need to share with our young people and with *ourselves*.

Of course the irony here is inescapable. No matter what we invest, all the money, time, and effort in the world can't make us look like George Clooney if we were born looking like Homer Simpson. And all the wrinkle cream under heaven will not stop the porcelain skin of the world's most gorgeous cover girl from eventually turning to the appearance of a weathered prune.

If we instead concern ourselves with attaining beauty of the heart, we can, through an ongoing relationship with Christ, grow more and more in his likeness. Although aging is inevitable, as our external self is growing less attractive, our internal self—the one that determines our eternity—can be growing ever more beautiful with every passing day through devotion and commitment to Jesus.

When we see ourselves through the eyes of Christ instead of through the eyes of a superficial, judgmental world, we can begin to view ourselves in a new light. It's a light that redefines beauty in terms of service and sacrifice, a light that says to the world that there's something more important, deeper, and more profound alive in our hearts. With his light shining through us, our very being is transformed. Not only do we see ourselves differently, but others do as well. The beauty of Christ alive within us is more attractive than the most expensive cosmetics money can buy, and you don't have to spend fifteen minutes taking it off with cold cream at the end of the day!

So how beautiful are we? We have been made in the image of God. How much more beautiful does it get?

A Closer Connection

How are you seeking to grow more and more like Christ every day? Do you spend more time preening for the world's acceptance or praying for the Lord's leading in your life? How many of your priorities are things that would make you beautiful in Jesus' eyes?

A Challenge and . . .

Since God chose you to be the holy people whom he loves, you must clothe yourselves with tenderhearted mercy, kindness, humility, gentleness, and patience. . . . And the most important piece of clothing you must wear is love. Love is what binds us all together in perfect harmony. COLOSSIANS 3:12-14

A Promise

We have stopped evaluating others by what the world thinks about them. . . . What this means is that those who become Christians become new persons. They are not the same anymore, for the old life has gone. A new life has begun!
2 CORINTHIANS 5:16-17

I Belong to Jesus!

Written by Dennis Jernigan
Recorded by Dennis Jernigan
From the 1995 Dove Nominee for Praise and Worship Album of the Year

Satan goes around like a roaring lion
Seeking whom he may devour
But he has been defeated so I'm testifyin'
By the blood of Jesus he lost power
Christ was lifted up with my sin upon Him
His life and blood came flowing down
So hear me I'm declaring Jesus Christ is Lord
I'm taking back His holy ground

CHORUS
I belong to Jesus
I belong to Him
I belong to Jesus
Free from sin
I belong to Jesus
I belong to Him
I belong to Jesus
Free from sin

All sin was nailed to the cross and the Lamb's blood flowing
Meant victory was sealed that day
When Satan saw the blood he knew that Christ had won it
And he knew that Sunday was on its way
The ground began to quake and all of
Heaven's power came bursting from the tomb within
The stone was rolled away and hell was overpowered
By the King who rose again

He was lifted up
He paid a costly price
He bought me with the blood of His own life
Christ the King now reigning
He wears the victor's crown
Satan was defeated when the blood flowed down

I BELONG TO JESUS!
A Heavenly Club

Indulge me for a moment. Take out your wallet. If you're like most people, you've got a lot of cards in there: You've probably got an auto club membership card in case of road emergencies, a couple of debit or credit cards for restaurants and store purchases, a couple of gasoline company cards, a library card, a medical insurance card, and a discount membership card from your local supermarket.

You might also have an airline frequent flyer card, a phone company long distance card, a hotel discount card, and a club card for one of the major wholesale buying clubs.

Where else are you a member? Well, since you're reading this book, you are probably a member of a church. If you have kids, you might be a member of the PTA. If you live in a modern subdivision, you're a member of a homeowners association. You get the point!

Like it or not, everything we belong to defines us to some extent.

People make assumptions and draw conclusions about us,

both good and bad, based upon the organizations with which we are affiliated and the groups to which we belong.

The question is, of the many things we are committed to and involved in, which one defines us the most? Nothing should define Christians more than their relationship with Jesus. It should be obvious to everyone we meet—not just to our family and friends but also to casual acquaintances and even total strangers—that we belong to Jesus! When we belong to Jesus, we should radiate a light and kindness that makes it clear whose we are. Love, forgiveness, and compassion should motivate our actions and shape our prayers. Our hope and joy should overflow, spilling onto those around us. People should want to know what club we belong to and how they can get in!

I'm not talking about church membership here. Church membership is fine, but being on a roster somewhere is not going to get us into heaven. In Matthew 7:22-23 Jesus says, "On judgment day many will tell me, 'Lord, Lord we prophesied in your name and cast out demons in your name and performed many miracles in your name.' But I will reply, 'I never knew you.'" Doubtless, there will be some church members who will find themselves falling into this category. We can't let our emphasis on joining a church overshadow our need for an active, ongoing personal relationship with Jesus Christ. We must never allow our church membership to lull us into becoming complacent Christians.

It's great to feel like we belong. Everybody needs to have a feeling of being accepted, being part of a community. So go ahead. Join the YMCA. Renew your membership in your hobby club. Enjoy your Thursday night bowling league. And by all means, belong to a good church and stay involved! But *never* substitute any activity or organization for a vibrant relationship with Jesus.

Remember, the only membership roll we want to make sure we're on is the Lamb's Book of Life!

A Closer Connection

Make a list of all the different entities you belong to. What about the way you live your life and your affiliations would make it obvious to everyone that you belong, first and foremost, to Christ?

A Challenge and . . .

Without wavering, let us hold tightly to the hope we say we have, for God can be trusted to keep his promise.   HEBREWS 10:23

A Promise

All who are victorious will be clothed in white. I will never erase their names from the Book of Life, but I will announce before my Father and his angels that they are mine.
REVELATION 3:5

I Pledge Allegiance to the Lamb

Written by Ray Boltz
Recorded by Ray Boltz
1995 Dove Inspirational Recorded Song of the Year

CHORUS
I pledge allegiance to the Lamb
With all my strength with all I am
I will seek to honor His commands
I pledge allegiance to the Lamb

I have heard how Christians long ago
Were brought before a tyrant's throne
They were told that he would spare their lives
If they would renounce the name of Christ
But one by one they chose to die
The Son of God they would not deny
Like a great angelic choir sings
I can almost hear their voices ring

CHORUS

Now the years have come and the years have gone
And the cause of Jesus still goes on
Now our time has come to count the cost
To reject this world to embrace the cross
And one by one let us live our lives
For the One who died to give us life
Till the trumpet sounds on the final day
Let us proudly stand and boldly say

To the Lamb of God who bore my pain
Who took my place who wore my shame
I will seek to honor His commands
I pledge allegiance to the Lamb

I PLEDGE ALLEGIANCE
TO THE LAMB
With Salvation and Justice for All

Anyone who grew up in the United States of America has said the Pledge of Allegiance. You probably learned it at school when you were a small child. Every morning after the first bell we would stand and recite the words pledging allegiance—unyielding loyalty and commitment—to our flag and our country.

This land we live in is a wonderful place, and we should take pride in it and be committed to making it the best it can be. The fact that we are able to practice our religion without fear of recrimination is our greatest liberty. However, like any institution of man, our country is a flawed place. America, the ideal, is a beautiful, shining beacon of liberty and justice for all. America, the reality, is a flesh-and-blood place where human beings struggle to rise above the greed, prejudice, and other conditions of our sinful nature.

The apostle Paul reminds us in 1 Corinthians 6:19-20, "You do not belong to yourself, for God bought you with a high price. So you must honor God."

In the end there's only One to whom we should pledge

allegiance—One who is over and above all, One who deserves our loyalty and commitment above those whom we hold dear, above family and country—Jesus Christ.

Most of us who confess Christ as our Lord know what that commitment looks like in our hearts. Sometimes though, it's hard to know how that allegiance should manifest itself in our day-to-day lives. Furthermore, in modern America, where we are not asked to defend our faith to the death, it's hard to know just how far our allegiance might go if put to the test.

Let me share with you an example of profound allegiance to Christ lived out. In the seventeenth century the King of Scotland made all of his subjects pledge their unswerving allegiance to him, insisting that they deny any other convictions, especially faith in Christ. He brutally persecuted all who resisted. A group that came to be known as the Scottish Covenanters resisted anyway, refusing to deny their Lord. In return, many of them were murdered, often in front of their own families.

One particularly inspiring story is that of the two Margarets. Margaret Wilson, eighteen, was imprisoned for refusing to drink to the health of the king. Margaret MacLachlan, a seventy-year-old widow, was jailed for praying with her family. The two women became friends during the three months they were incarcerated together. Then they were sentenced to death by drowning. They were tied to stakes at low tide, the elder Margaret further out presumably so that the younger woman would see her drown and be compelled to switch her allegiance to the king. The strategy did not work.

When the water was up to young Margaret's neck, the persecutors asked her to "pray for the king as he is supreme over all persons and causes, ecclesiastic as well as civil." She refused, and they held her head under water for a short while, then lifted her up again. "Pray for the king!" they demanded. From the shore her family and friends pleaded with her to change her mind, but she wouldn't. She prayed instead, "Lord give the king repentance, forgiveness, and salvation, if it be Thy holy will." The dragoon in charge grew livid and demanded she swear allegiance to the king. "No! No! No sinful oaths for me. I am one of Christ's children. Let me go!" With that, they brutally held her head under the water until she drowned.

It may be hard to imagine such a scene happening in your neighborhood. But the profound faith exhibited by these two women calls each of us to examine our commitment to Christ. How different our country might look today if Christians in America took their faith as seriously as the two Margarets took theirs. How different would our world be if Christians everywhere served Christ before country?

A Closer Connection
What does your allegiance to Christ cost you in your life? How many times have you kept silent about Christ in a situation to avoid being uncomfortable?

A Challenge and . . .
If you want to be my follower you must love me more than your own father and mother, wife and children, brothers and sisters—yes, more than your own life. Otherwise, you cannot be my disciple. LUKE 14:26

A Promise
If anyone acknowledges me publicly here on earth, I will openly acknowledge that person before my Father in heaven. MATTHEW 10:32

I Surrender All

Words and Music by David Moffitt and Regie Hamm
Recorded by Clay Crosse
1994 Dove Nominee for Song of the Year

I have wrestled in the darkness of this lonely pilgrim land
Raising strong and mighty fortresses that I alone command
But these castles I've constructed by the strength
of my own hand
Are just temporary kingdoms on foundations made of sand
In the middle of the battle I believe I've fin'lly found
I'll never know the thrill of vict'ry till I'm willin'
to lay down
All my weapons of defense and earthly strategies of war
So I'm layin' down my arms and runnin' helplessly to Yours

CHORUS
I surrender all my silent hopes and dreams
Though the price to follow costs me everything
I surrender all my human soul desires
If sacrifice requires that all my kingdoms fall
I surrender all

If the source of my ambition is the treasure I obtain
If I measure my success on a scale of earthly gain
If the focus of my vision is the status I attain
My accomplishments are worthless and my efforts are in vain
So I lay aside these trophies to pursue a higher crown
And should You choose somehow to use the life
I willingly lay down
I surrender all the triumph for it's only by Your grace
I relinquish all the glory I surrender all the praise

CHORUS

Everything I am all I've done and all I've known
Now belongs to You
The life I live is not my own
Just as Abraham laid Isaac on the sacrificial fire
If all I have is all that You desire
I surrender all
Let all my kingdoms fall
I surrender all

I SURRENDER ALL
What's in the Way?

Who of us can remember horsing around as a child and getting caught in some kind of wrestling hold having to cry out, "Uncle!" to be set free? Or maybe it's easier for you to remember somebody sitting on you and tickling you until you laughed so hard it hurt, begging for mercy. In either event, you were anxious to surrender. You weren't worried about pride or saving face. All you wanted was to be set free and you would do anything, no matter how embarrassing—even cry "Uncle!"—to make it happen.

The same children who found it so easy to surrender grow up to be adults who find it hard to surrender *anything*. We want it all, and we want it *our way*. We think our way is the "right" way. We convince ourselves that we're in control when in reality we don't even control whether or not our hearts will take their next beat. In America we've even managed to delude ourselves into thinking we "deserve" certain amenities—a college education, a great job, a beautiful home, a nice car—confusing desires with rights, and necessities with privileges.

As Christians we're familiar with the story of the rich young ruler in Mark 10:17-22. He comes to Jesus and asks what he must do to get eternal life. Jesus responds, "You know the commandments."

The young man replies that he has obeyed all the commandments since he was a child. Then Jesus says, "You lack only one thing. Go and sell all you have and give the money to the poor, and you will have treasure in heaven. Then come, follow me."

The young man went away sad because he had many possessions. He couldn't surrender it all even after meeting Jesus face-to-face!

Most of us read that story and justify not doing what Jesus asks this young man to do because *we* aren't rich. But by what standard are we making that determination? There are people in third world countries whose annual salary wouldn't be enough to purchase this book!

You may have heard the "Give 5" national radio campaign trying to get Americans to commit 5 percent of their income to charitable causes. Not only are we not giving all—we're having trouble giving a fraction!

But surrendering is not only about money and possessions. Christ wants us to surrender *anything* that gets in the way of our relationship with him. Even family.

"Do you think I have come to bring peace to the earth?" Jesus asks in Luke 12:51. "No, I have come to bring strife and division! From now on families will be split apart, three in favor of me, and two against—or the other way around."

There can be nothing standing in the way of our relationship with Christ. We must lay down all our idols, wherever we find them. This is not easy. It's revolutionary. It's countercultural. But as Christians our passion should be to see our will conformed to that of Christ. We need to give him our hopes and our dreams, our strengths and our weaknesses, our successes and our failures, our joys and our burdens, our time and our money. We must surrender all.

It's only then, in sweet divine irony, that by surrendering all to him, he will give us back a more abundant life than we ever dreamed possible.

A Closer Connection

What types of things have you made idols in your life? What is keeping you from surrendering all to Jesus Christ and making him Lord of your life?

A Challenge and . . .

Dear children, keep away from anything that might take God's place in your hearts. 1 JOHN 5:21

A Promise

If you try to keep your life for yourself, you will lose it. But if you give up your life for me, you will find true life. LUKE 9:24

I've Just Seen Jesus

Written by Bill and Gloria Gaither and Danny Daniels
Recorded by Sandy Patty and Larnelle Harris
From the 1986 Dove Inspirational Album of the Year

We knew He was dead
"It is finished," He'd said
We had watched as His life ebbed away
Then we all stood around 'til the guards took Him down
Joseph begged for His body that day
It was late afternoon when we got to the tomb
Wrapped His body in grave clothes and spice
We laid Him to rest, He had given His best
He had loved us and paid a big price but

CHORUS
I've just seen Jesus I tell you He's alive!
I've just seen Jesus
Our precious Lord, alive!
And I knew He really saw me too
As if 'til now I'd never lived
All that I've done before won't matter anymore
I've just seen Jesus
I've just seen Jesus
And I'll never be the same again

It was just before dawn I was running along
Barely able to see where to go
For the tears in my eyes and the dusky sunrise
Seemed to cloud up my vision so
It was His voice I heard first those kind gentle words
Asking what was my reason for tears
And I sobbed in despair, "My Lord is not there!"
He said, "Child! It is I. I am here!"

Just a regular day I was making my way
Down the road in the dust and the heat
Not much on my mind wasn't trying to find
A purposeful path for my feet
Just a regular day neither sunny nor grey
And I'd learned to expect nothing more
I thought dreams were for fools and I knew all the rules
I heard empty statements before

Then I saw Jesus
I tell you He's alive!
I've just seen Jesus
My precious Lord alive!
And I knew He really saw me too
And until now I've never lived!
All that I've done before won't matter anymore
I've just seen Jesus
I've just seen Jesus
And I'll never be the same again

I'VE JUST SEEN JESUS
The Ever-Present Lord

Once when I was in a baseball stadium parking lot there was a man with a cardboard sign and a megaphone. Jesus Is Coming Soon the sign proclaimed. He shouted into the megaphone and waved the sign, apparently unheeded by the crowd of fifty thousand pouring out of the stadium. You've probably seen them, too—people with doomsday signs proclaiming the end of the world or faded billboards along the interstate in between ads for the Burger Barn and the Best Rest Motel.

The message is always the same. Repent before it's too late. And you know what? We need to do that. Repentance is a good idea. It's a really good idea.

We *should* all repent and place our trust in the saving Christ. However, when we focus on the fact that Jesus is coming *some*day, we miss the truth of the matter that he comes to us *every* day.

If we stop to think about it for a moment, we realize there are so many ways that Jesus comes to us through the Holy Spirit that they are almost too numerous to count. He comes to us privately. He comes to us when we pray. He comes to us in the stillness and contemplation of our devotional time. He comes to us in the quiet reading and study of the Scriptures.

He comes to us corporately. He comes to us through the inspired preaching of his Word by committed pastors and in the sacred, classic songs of the faith as sung by gifted soloists and choirs. He comes to us as we praise and worship him together. He comes to us in the reenactment of his birth at Christmastime and again in the reenactment of his passion at Easter.

Perhaps more important, he comes to us in one another. Sometimes he comes in a smile or the kind word of a stranger or the helping hands of a friend.

And *sometimes* he comes as the person in *need* of a smile or the kind word of a stranger or the helping hands of a friend.

Then there are the unexpected ways that Jesus comes to us:

- In a homeless man asleep in an alleyway Dumpster clutching a bottle of whiskey.
- In a crack-addicted mother, pregnant with her third unwanted child, selling whatever is at her disposal to feed her habit.

- In a ninety-five-year-old woman sitting in a wheelchair with drool trickling down her chin, staring vacantly across the room, unable to remember her own name.

Each of these was created in the image of God. And as Jesus tells us in Matthew 25:40, "I assure you, when you did it to one of the least of these my brothers and sisters, you were doing it to me!"

Wouldn't it be wonderful if just for a moment you could be transported back in time to the resurrection of our Lord? It would have been so exciting to be there to see him—to have been able to run through the streets shouting, "He's alive! I tell you, our Lord is alive!"

The knowledge that Christ faced death for all of us and emerged victorious from the grave should be cause for us to live lives of unbounded joy, committed to him in all we do. He has given us a blueprint for how to express that joy. He has told us how to show him the love that we have for him.

It's when we share that love with "the least of these" that we see Jesus—who is old and young, rich and poor, black and white, male and female—each and every day of our lives.

I've just seen Jesus. I tell you he's alive. He is our ever-present Lord. He's as close as our next prayer and as close as the next person we meet. Let us love him through the way we love each other.

A Closer Connection

How can you treat everyone you meet as if you were doing it to the Lord? How might your relationships look different if you looked for Jesus in your family members? your neighbors? your friends? your enemies?

A Challenge and . . .

Continue to love each other with true Christian love. Don't forget to show hospitality to strangers, for some who have done this have entertained angels without realizing it! HEBREWS 13:1-2

A Promise

Those who obey my commandments are the ones who love me. And because they love me, my Father will love them, and I will love them. And I will reveal myself to each one of them. JOHN 14:21

I Will Follow Christ

Words and Music by Clay Crosse and Steve Siler
Recorded by Clay Crosse (with Bob Carlisle and Bebe Winans)
2000 Dove Inspirational Song of the Year

The twelve of you walked on this earth together
The Father was a brother to you all
The teaching that you heard was the Living Word
The wonders and the miracles you saw

There were times of awesome inspiration
There were times you didn't understand
When He had to go and you felt alone
It must've been so hard to see His plan
I think about the way you carried on
In the face of persecution you stood strong so

CHORUS
Yes, I will follow Christ
I will run the race
Fighting the good fight
Standing on my faith
I will wear the name of Jesus
I will give Him all my life
As for me no matter what the sacrifice
I will follow Christ

I don't have to look across the ages
His voice is speaking in my heart today
His word is like a flame consuming all my shame
His life a shining star to show the way

146

I behold Your life and see the man You want me to become
Living like someone whose heart belongs to the kingdom that
was sealed on Calvary
I will show the world what I believe

I WILL FOLLOW CHRIST
Out of Your Comfort Zone?

Have you ever been asked to do a job you didn't feel capable
of doing? a task that would take you out of your comfort
zone?

All of us have had such challenges sometime in life—if not
now. Whether it's training a new coworker, speaking before
a group, planning an event, or talking with someone about
your faith, such tasks are indeed stretching. So when
presented with the opportunity, it's not surprising that we
feel anxious, incompetent, and perhaps even a little terrified.
Who wouldn't?

Jesus' original twelve disciples must have felt the same
way at times. After all, they too were human beings. Even
though they had Jesus—in person—walking alongside them
doing miracles in front of their eyes, at times they didn't
understand fully who he was or what his purpose on earth
was. The disciples' humanity emerges again and again in
Scripture. The stories reveal multiple emotions—excitement,
terror, pride, shame, joy, and devastation. Other stories show
that sometimes these men were effective and other times
incompetent (in other words, a lot like us today!). And yet,

after Jesus' crucifixion and resurrection, these oh-so-human disciples demonstrated incredible faith, even to the point of risking their lives.

What more compelling evidence could there be than that the disciples *knew,* without a doubt, they had been in the presence of God when Christ was with them? And later, when Jesus appeared to them after the Resurrection, the disciples became filled with the Holy Spirit and went forth boldly spreading the gospel and establishing the church.

Did the original disciples have it easy? Certainly not. They lived in a time and place where it was dangerous to even mention the name of Christ. They were persecuted, and some were even killed for their faith in Jesus. Their "job"—spreading the good news about Jesus Christ to the world—was certainly overwhelming and took them out of their comfort zone.

Today, if you've accepted Christ as the Son of God, you, too, have received the Holy Spirit to guide you. And you, too, have a new "job"—to carry on the work that the original disciples started. That means not only telling people about Christ and the difference he makes in your life but also choosing to follow Christ in your daily decisions, whether large or small.

Although you don't need to fear being killed for your faith (at least not in America), you still face persecution: people who make fun of your Christian views, a boss who won't promote you because you "have faith," "friends" who talk about you and your "integrity" behind your back.

In addition, you face a very noisy, very busy world in which many things compete for your attention, blocking the Holy Spirit's guidance. Even the good things—like family, community, career—can hold back your decision to follow Christ with your whole heart.

But Jesus' words in Scripture are piercingly clear: He must be number one in your life. How can you make sure you're giving Jesus all of your life and not just a part? Continually strive to follow him in each thought you think, each word you speak, and each action you take. Ask him to be at work in your heart, revealing areas where you need to change to become more Christlike. For if you do so, then your actions will reflect not only your own personal faith but the love of God to your family, neighborhood, workplace, community, and the world.

A Closer Connection

Have you given Jesus your *entire* life or just a part? Do you turn each decision over to him? How is it clear to others that you belong to Jesus—no matter the sacrifice?

A Challenge and . . .

Let us run with endurance the race that God has set before us. We do this by keeping our eyes on Jesus, on whom our faith depends from start to finish. HEBREWS 12:1-2

A Promise

I have fought a good fight, I have finished the race, and I have remained faithful. And now the prize awaits me—the crown of righteousness that the Lord, the righteous Judge, will give me on that great day of his return. 2 TIMOTHY 4:7-8

In Christ Alone

Written by Shawn Craig and Don Koch
Recorded by Michael English
1994 Dove Song of the Year

In Christ alone will I glory
Though I could pride myself in battles won
For I've been blessed beyond measure
And by His strength alone I overcome
Oh I could stop and count successes
Like diamonds in my hand
But those trophies could not equal
To the grace by which I stand

CHORUS
In Christ alone I place my trust
And find my glory in the power of the cross
In every victory let it be said of me
My source of strength
My source of hope
Is Christ alone

In Christ alone will I glory
For only by His grace I am redeemed
And only His tender mercy
Could reach beyond my weakness to my need
Now I seek no greater honor
Than just to know Him more
And to count my gains but losses
To the glory of my Lord

IN CHRIST ALONE

Where the Good Gifts Come From

Have you ever known someone who was truly humble—someone who was *always* more interested in talking about you than in talking about himself? At the first church my wife and I attended after we were married there was a man named Bill Thomas who was just such a person. Every time someone went up to Bill, he had him talking about himself within ten seconds. Then one day he was cast as one of the lead actors in a network TV series. *Aha!* I thought. *Here's my chance to get Bill to talk about himself!* The next time I saw Bill at church I raced over to congratulate him and hear all about it. He artfully deflected the compliment and within thirty seconds flat he had me talking about myself again.

"Oh, Lord, it's hard to be humble." So goes the old Mac Davis song. It's true. We all like to take credit for our accomplishments and be acknowledged when we've done something well. It's the most amazing thing though. If we're the ones doing the acknowledging, it can be curiously unsatisfying. Even worse, when we toot our own horn, it begins to sound like bragging, and soon our boorish behavior has essentially cancelled out whatever we were praising ourselves for in the first place!

As Christians we should never brag about ourselves because we know Someone else who is worthy of being bragged about. It's in Christ that we find perfect strength. It's in Christ that we find perfect love. Everything that we have and everything that we are come from him. Why would we spend even five seconds talking about our own goodness when we could spend it pointing people to the One who is truly good?

In Matthew 6:3 Jesus says, "Don't tell your left hand what

your right hand is doing." He is saying that we should not be concerned with taking credit for doing good works. The joy is in the doing itself. When we stop to pat ourselves on the back, we have one less hand to use to serve Christ. Besides, we can't take the credit and be giving it to Jesus at the same time.

Jesus also warns us to be careful about doing our good deeds in the public eye.

"Give your gifts in secret, and your Father, who knows all secrets, will reward you" (Matthew 6:4). Amazing! God knows our hearts and our minds. He knows our motivations. If our motivation is our own self-aggrandizement, it isn't going to do us any good on a spiritual plane. Whatever reward the world has to offer will be our *only* reward. However, when our motivation comes from serving Christ and sharing his message with the world, we are less likely to be needy, selfish, attention-craving people. Heaven's applause will matter more to us than the applause of people when we consider it our greatest honor to live in complete submission to the perfect will of God.

Hey, we're all human. I'm not suggesting that you have to feel guilty when someone pays you a nice compliment. As a matter of fact, there's great power in the words we speak to each other, and we should always seek to uplift those around us with positive, affirming comments and be gracious when we are on the receiving end of such attention. But we should never forget where all good gifts come from and take every opportunity to publicly acknowledge that it is in and through Christ that we are able to reach out to others with the best that is in us.

A Closer Connection

Have you ever taken the credit for something Christ has done in your life? What gifts has he given you that have allowed

you to look good in the world's eyes? What are some ways
you could give God the credit for those gifts?

A Challenge and . . .

*Those who exalt themselves will be humbled, and those who
humble themselves will be exalted.*   MATTHEW 23:12

A Promise

*The person who wishes to boast should boast only of what the
Lord has done.*   I CORINTHIANS 1:31

A Yes
B The gift to love & care for babies
   & toddlers. I am able to communicate 'k them & also he has given
   me patience & endurance.
   I can give God the credit by
   @ telling others its a God given gift
   to glorify Him in my life

Jesus Freak

Words and Music by Mark Heimermann and Kevin McKeehan
Recorded by dc Talk
1996 Dove Song of the Year

Separated I cut myself clean
From a past that comes back in my darkest of dreams
Been apprehended by a spiritual force
And a grace that replaced all the me I've divorced
I saw a man with a tattoo on his big fat belly
It wiggled around like marmalade jelly
It took me a while to catch what it said
'Cause I had to match the rhythm of his belly with my head
Jesus saves is what it raved in a typical tattoo green
He stood on a box in the middle of the city
And he claimed he had a dream

CHORUS
What will people think when they hear that I'm a Jesus freak
What will people do when they find that it's true
I don't really care if they label me a Jesus freak
'Cause there ain't no disguising the truth

Kamikaze my death is gain
I've been marked by my Maker a peculiar display
The high and lofty they see me as weak
'Cause I won't live and die by the power they seek
There was a man from the desert with naps in his head
The sand that he walked was also his bed
The words that he spoke made the people assume
There wasn't too much left in the upper room
With skins on his back and hair on his face
They thought he was strange by the locusts he ate
The Pharisee's tripped when they heard him speak
Until the king took the head of this Jesus freak

People say I'm strange does it make me a stranger
That my best friend was born in a manger
People say I'm strange does it make me a stranger
That my best friend was born in a manger

What will people think (What will people think)
What will people do (What will people do)
I don't really care (What else can I say)
There ain't no disguising the truth

JESUS FREAK
When Normal's Not Enough

In the 1970s a group of vocal followers of Christ were labeled
"Jesus Freaks." It was meant to be a derisive put-down. Of
course, anyone who is head over heels in love with Jesus
wouldn't care about being called a silly name. This refresh-
ing lyric is a playful tribute to those in our recent faith
history who weren't afraid to be labeled as freaks for their
faith, turning an epithet into a compliment.

However, it also challenges us to think about how far
outside the lines we are willing to go in the name of Jesus.
Are we willing to be demeaned as kooks for Christ?

When you think about it, if we were to take Christ seriously and act upon his word, people would think we were
more than a little crazy. "Bless those who curse you, do
good to those who hate you," Jesus says in Matthew 5:44
(NKJV). In our world when someone curses you, "normal"
is to trade insults in an escalating game of verbal one-
upmanship. As for people who hate us, "normal" is either
to avoid them, talk about them behind their backs, or

scheme against them. Pray for our enemies? That's pretty freaky stuff!

"If you are slapped on the right cheek, turn the other, too," Jesus instructs in Matthew 5:39. In our world, "normal" is when shoved, shove back. When slugged, slug back. Only a coward fails to respond to physical aggression.

This is Playground Survival 101 taught to little boys everywhere in America and offered up as foreign policy by our political leaders. The conventional wisdom would make cowards out of abnormal folks like Gandhi and Martin Luther King Jr.

Not strike back? Again, pretty freaky stuff!

"Don't store up treasures here on earth," Jesus intones in Matthew 6:19. Oh, come on now, this is going just a little too far, isn't it? It's "normal" to want nice things. You work hard. You deserve lots of nice stuff. What's wrong with a beautiful, spacious home, a nice wardrobe, a couple of SUVs, and a healthy, expanding financial portfolio? What's wrong with collecting fine art or valuable antiques?

Hey, I didn't say it. Jesus did! I think it has something to do with knowing that after a while our possessions start to own us instead of the other way around.

Mess with our comfort? Divest instead of acquire? Totally freaky stuff!

Even if someone "wrongs you seven times a day and each time turns again and asks forgiveness, forgive him," Jesus tells us in Luke 17:4. "Normal" in our world would be to hold a grudge. Make 'em sweat. They're feeling guilty. In our passive-aggressive society you can use that as currency. Of course, what we fail to realize is that holding on to that leverage requires that we nurse and cultivate our anger, imprisoning ourselves in the process. Not make somebody pay for the wrong they've done you? Just forgive, just like that?! Pretty freaky stuff!

Of course we're not called out on this limb of freakiness individually. We are called to be a *community* of freaks. Listen to the first-century church in Acts 4:32-35: "All the believers were of one heart and mind, and they felt that what they owned was not their own. . . . There was no poverty among them, because people who owned land or houses sold them and brought the money to the apostles to give to others in need." Pretty freaky stuff indeed.

So if somebody calls you a Jesus Freak, smile. It means you're taking the Savior seriously and it's showing up in your life. On the other hand, if nobody's insulted you in the name of Jesus recently, it's probably time to do something *ab*normal for the cause of Christ.

A Closer Connection

Is your faithfulness to Christ causing you to stand out from the crowd? What kinds of things have you done lately that an unbeliever might have found a little nutty? Pray for God to show you new ways to be *ab*normal for him.

A Challenge and . . .

You must put aside your selfish ambition, shoulder your cross, and follow me.   MARK 8:34

A Promise

God blesses those who are persecuted because they live for God, for the Kingdom of Heaven is theirs.   MATTHEW 5:10

Jesus King of Angels

Written by Fernando Ortega
Recorded by Fernando Ortega
2000 Dove Nominee for Inspirational Recorded Song of the Year

Jesus King of angels
Heaven's light
Shine Your face upon this house tonight
Let no evil come into my dreams
Light of heaven keep me in Your peace

Remind me how You made dark spirits flee
And spoke Your power to the raging sea
And spoke Your mercy to a sinful man
Remind me Jesus for this is what I am

CHORUS
The universe is vast beyond the stars
But You are mindful when a sparrow falls
And mindful of the anxious thoughts that find me
Surround me and bind me

With all my heart I love You sov'reign Lord
Tomorrow let me love You even more
And rise to speak the goodness of Your name
Until I close my eyes in sleep again

CHORUS

Jesus King of angels
Heaven's light
Hold my hand and keep me through the night

JESUS KING OF ANGELS
A Lullaby for the Big Kids

Several times throughout the years my dad has said to me words to the effect of, "You know, Son, even though you grow older and look older to other people, you never stop feeling young on the inside. It's only when you look in the mirror that you say, 'Hey, who is that old guy?'"

Now that I'm a little older myself I'm beginning to understand what he means.

Everybody in the world expects me to behave like an adult. My kids think I know stuff because I'm their dad. Younger songwriters think I have all the answers simply because I've had songs recorded. I'm asked to make responsible business decisions by my colleagues. The world expects me to pay bills and manage a household with all the maturity and command that suggests. There's only one problem. There's a huge part of me that still feels like I'm about seventeen. Some days I just want to scream, "You've got the wrong guy! I'm not grown up enough yet to handle this!" People call me Mr. Siler, and sometimes I still turn around to see if my dad is in the room.

Yes, if we're honest, we all will admit that there is still a little kid in there. Some of us are more in denial about it than others. But the truth is we're all just overgrown kids. For some of us it just depends what day it is or how things are going. No matter how often you feel that way, whenever you do there is some great news to remember.

We are *all* children of God. When the disciples tried to shoo children away from Jesus in Mark 10:14-15, he said, "Let the children come to me. Don't stop them! For the Kingdom of God belongs to such as these. I assure you, anyone who doesn't have their kind of faith will never get into the Kingdom of God."

Jesus is telling us to stay in touch with our childlike side.

Keep our sense of wonder. Don't be jaded. Stay in touch with our innocence. Think about it. Kids aren't born with prejudice. They learn it from adults. Trust people. Be happy. Have faith. It might seem cooler to be seen as cynical and sophisticated by the world, but that's the lazy way out. Anybody can be a downer. It actually takes more discipline to be loving and encouraging.

So if we're going to acknowledge that there is still a kid inside of us, it's going to follow that we're going to need someone to "sing" us to sleep once in a while. With this wonderful lyric, Fernando Ortega has offered up just such imagery. We are allowed to see ourselves for the children of God that we are and rest in that.

Jesus is the light shining down a protective covering over our home while we sleep. Jesus is the One standing guard over our dreams. The Jesus who commanded the storms to be quiet and who cast out demons is the author of our peace. Jesus is the One who is aware of each and every one of us and every grown-up thought that assails us.

We are his precious children. He loved us enough to die for us. He *loves* us enough to be present with us through his Spirit, day and night. We don't have to be strong or smart all the time. Like children, we don't have to have all the answers because we know the One who does. We can sleep in peace. Jesus is awake.

With that kind of assurance why wouldn't we rise up in the morning ready to speak the goodness of his name?

A Closer Connection

What are some activities that you enjoyed as a child? Listen carefully to some of the children around you. What are they seeing that you've been too busy to notice? Pray for a child-like spirit.

A Challenge and . . .

Then he said, "I assure you, unless you turn from your sins and become as little children, you will never get into the Kingdom of Heaven."   MATTHEW 18:3

A Promise

See how very much our heavenly Father loves us, for he allows us to be called his children, and we really are!   1 JOHN 3:1

Jesus Will Still Be There

Words and Music by John Mandeville and Robert Sterling
Recorded by Point of Grace
1995 Dove Nominee for Inspirational Recorded Song of the Year

Things change
Plans fail
You look for love on a grander scale
Storms rise
Hopes fade
And you place your bets on another day
When the going gets tough
When the ride's too rough
When you're just not sure enough

CHORUS
Jesus will still be there
His love will never change
Sure as a steady rain
Jesus will still be there
When no one else is true
He'll still be lovin' you
When it looks like you've lost it all
And you haven't got a prayer
Jesus will still be there

Time flies
Hearts turn
A little bit wiser from lessons learned
But sometimes
Weakness wins
And you lose your foothold once again
When the going gets tough

When the ride's too rough
When you're just not sure enough

CHORUS

When it looks like you've lost it all
And you haven't got a prayer
Jesus will still be there

JESUS WILL STILL BE THERE
Wherever You Go, There You Are

Everybody loves a winner. Nowhere is that more true than in America. Madison Avenue knows this. That's why Nike offered Tiger Woods millions of dollars to wear their logo at his golf tournaments. Winning athletes sell. Remember Mark Spitz, the first to wear a milk mustache? Or how about Michael Jordan soaring across a Wheaties box? From tennis shoes to breakfast cereals, if Mr. or Ms. Current Champion says he or she likes it, then we like it, too. We want to be on the winning side. It's just human nature.

There's nothing wrong with wanting to be a winner is there? After all, winners usually have a positive attitude. They're happy and successful, or at least they appear to be. They've got money and maybe a little bit of fame. They've got the good life—and the good stuff! People like to be around them. We're taught that success breeds success.

Winners have things going their way, and we want a little of that to rub off on us. We want to be in the in crowd and have everybody love us. There's only one little problem with things going our way though. As Dr. Seuss says in *Oh the Places You'll Go,* "Sometimes they *won't!*"

And when that happens, we may discover that we have some fair-weather friends. We've all heard the expression. We've probably even all had a few—people who we thought really cared about us who suddenly didn't seem to be around when things started not to go our way.

Maybe you had an exciting new business idea you were working on. Everybody was really excited about it in the planning stage. It seemed like you couldn't lose. But one day you looked up and suddenly realized something was terribly wrong. Overnight all the people who had wanted a piece of the idea when it looked like a winner were gone.

Or perhaps you were working on a school play or a church presentation. When it looked like it was going to be a big success, everybody wanted to share a piece of the credit with you. But when things got a little difficult and it didn't work out quite as planned, you wound up shouldering the blame all by yourself.

You may be going through some really trying circumstance in your life right now, something that has left you feeling totally abandoned by people you trusted and totally alone. You may have reached the point where you are so despondent you feel as if even God has abandoned you.

In any event, there is something you need to remember. Once you have accepted Jesus Christ into your heart, he is there with you *always* through the Holy Spirit. "He will give you mighty inner strength through his Holy Spirit" (Ephesians 3:16). You've heard the old expression "Wherever you go, there you are." Well, the same is true of Jesus. Wherever you go, there *he* is.

There's *no* situation, no matter how frightening or unfamiliar, no matter how challenging or overwhelming, that we have to face alone. Christ, through the Holy Spirit, indwells us and is present with us in *all* times and in *all* places.

Jesus isn't interested in our social status or our reputation. He's interested in our hearts. Let us not be so concerned with winning in the world that we forget that we have already won through Christ. Let us remember whose we are and rest in the knowledge that we are justified through his love for us and need never face anything alone.

We may want desperately to be popular. We may want desperately to succeed. We may want desperately to win. But even in the midst of our own personal desert, our failure, or our loss . . . Jesus will *still* be there.

A Closer Connection

What are some things you could be doing to move into a closer personal walk with the Savior? How much time do you spend talking to him daily in prayer, nurturing that closeness?

A Challenge and . . .

Those who obey God's commandments live in fellowship with him, and he with them. And we know he lives in us because the Holy Spirit lives in us. I JOHN 3:24

A Promise

Can anything ever separate us from Christ's love? Does it mean he no longer loves us if we have trouble or calamity, or are persecuted, or are hungry or cold or in danger or threatened with death? . . . No, despite all these things, overwhelming victory is ours through Christ, who loved us. ROMANS 8:35-37

King of Glory

Words and Music by Mac Powell and Third Day
Recorded by Third Day
From the 2001 Dove Praise and Worship Album

Who is this King of Glory
That pursues me with His love
And haunts me with each hearing
Of His softly spoken words
My conscience a reminder
Of forgiveness that I need
Who is this King of Glory who offers it to me

Who is this King of angels
Oh blessed Prince of Peace
Revealing things in heaven
And all its mysteries
My spirit's ever longing
For His grace in which to stand
Who is this King of Glory Son of God and Son of Man

CHORUS
His name is Jesus
Precious Jesus
The Lord Almighty
King of my heart
King of Glory

Who is this King of Glory
With strength and majesty
And wisdom beyond measure
The gracious King of kings
The Lord of earth and heaven
The Creator of all things
Who is this King of Glory
He's everything to me

Who is this King of Glory
He's everything to me

KING OF GLORY
The Majesty of Service

What do you think of when you think of glory? Perhaps a college football team winning the big game as in "win one for the Gipper!" Or maybe it's an Olympic athlete bringing glory to his or her home country by capturing a gold medal. The term is often used to describe exploits on the field of battle as demonstrated in the excellent 1989 Civil War film *Glory*.

As believers in the Lord Jesus Christ we might tend to think of other images when we hear the word *glory*—images like the one found in Luke 21:27: "Then everyone will see the Son of Man arrive on the clouds with power and great glory." In some Bible translations the word *glory* appears more than 250 times!

Contemporary Christian churches around the world seek to glorify Jesus. After all he has done for us this is a completely reasonable response. But what does Jesus think? How does Jesus himself see glory?

In John 8:50-54 Jesus says, "Though I have no wish to glorify myself, God wants to glorify me. Let him be the judge. . . . If I am merely boasting about myself, it doesn't count. But it is my Father who says these glorious things about me." Later, in John 14:13 he says, "You can ask for anything in my name, and I will do it, because the work of the Son brings glory to the Father." In John 15:8 Jesus says, "My true disciples produce much fruit. This brings great glory to my Father." And finally, in John 17:1 Jesus prays, "Father, the time has come. Glorify your Son so he can give glory back to you."

Clearly Christ is only concerned with glory insofar as it reflects upon God the Father. It is not surprising then that he, whose ministry was all about service and valuing others above oneself, would seek to have us give whatever honor we think is due him to his Father in heaven.

So how do we human beings get the opportunity to share in this glory? Again, not surprisingly, it's through service. Read the words of Jesus in Matthew 25:31-34. Jesus, "and all the angels with him," will sit "upon his glorious throne." Speaking to the righteous who have served others in his name Christ will say, "Come, you who are blessed by my Father, inherit the Kingdom prepared for you from the foundation of the world."

Where, besides in worship, is the glory of Christ to be found in our day-to-day lives?

Wherever we find ourselves. Jesus doesn't care if you're a plumber, a movie star, an auto mechanic, a stay-at-home mom, a schoolteacher, or an accountant. He cares about whether or not you love people. Glory on the racetrack or the basketball court is one thing. Glory in those settings means the adulation and applause of the world. The kind of glory that comes from ladling soup in a homeless shelter or visiting a nursing home means the applause of heaven.

So who is this King of Glory? He is the One who reigns forever at the right hand of his Father. He is the One who, just as he stooped to wash his disciples' feet, stoops to love a hurting world. He is as far away as heaven and as close as a prayer. He is the One who sacrificed his own life so that we might live forever.

He is the beginning and the end, which was, is, and always will be. He is Jesus Christ the Lord.

A Closer Connection

What are some of the ways you acknowledge the King of Glory? Pray for Christ's example to be made manifest in your worship and your service.

A Challenge and . . .

All glory to him, who alone is God our Savior, through Jesus Christ our Lord. Yes, glory, majesty, power, and authority belong to him, in the beginning, now, and forevermore. Amen.
JUDE 1:25

A Promise

For this is the secret: Christ lives in you, and this is your assurance that you will share in his glory. COLOSSIANS 1:27

Lord of the Dance

Words and Music by Steven Curtis Chapman and Scott Smith
Recorded by Steven Curtis Chapman
From the 1997 Dove Pop/Contemporary Album of the Year

On the bank of the Tennessee River
In a small Kentucky town
I drew my first breath one cold November morning
And before my feet even touched the ground
With the doctors and nurses gathered 'round
I started to dance
I started to dance

A little boy full of wide-eyed wonder
Footloose and fancy free
But it would happen as it does for every dancer
That I'd stumble on a truth I couldn't see
And find a longing deep inside of me it said

I am the heart I need the heartbeat
I am the eyes I need the sight
I realize that I am just a body
I need the life I move my feet
I go through the motions
But who'll give purpose to the chance
I am the dancer
I need the Lord of the dance

The world beneath us spins in circles
And this life makes us twist and turn and sway
But we were made for more than rhythm with no reason
By the One who moves with passion and with grace
As He dances over all that He has made

I am the heart He is the heartbeat
I am the eyes He is the sight

And I see clearly I am just a body
He is the life I move my feet
I go through the motions
But He gives purpose to chance
I am the dancer
He is the Lord of the dance

Lord of the dance, Lord of the dance
And while the music of His love and mercy plays
I will fall down on my knees and I will pray

I am the heart You are the heartbeat
I am the eyes You are the sight
And I see clearly I am just a body
You are the life I move my feet
I go through the motions
But You give purpose to chance
I am the dancer
You are the Lord of the dance
I am the dancer
You are the Lord of the dance

LORD OF THE DANCE
Meaning to Our Motion

Imagine an aspiring dancer auditioning for a part in a new Broadway show. He's practiced all his life, and this is his big chance. He goes to the initial audition, and he even gets asked back for a second look, and a third. Finally, he's waiting for the call that will tell him whether or not his dream will come true! Then the phone rings. He got the part! He's given a date and time to show up at the theater.

However, when he arrives at the theater, something is terribly wrong. The date he's been given is opening night! He hasn't had one bit of rehearsal. In the confusion backstage he comes to find out that none of the other dancers have had any rehearsal either. No one knows what he or she is supposed to do!

Then the production manager is shouting, "Places! Everybody onstage!"

The dancers scramble out onto the dark stage in total confusion. Where do they stand? What are their parts? The pit orchestra launches into the overture. Pretty soon the curtain begins to rise. It's time to dance!

But nobody knows the routine. All the dancers are trying to respond to what they are hearing in the music, but they are crashing and bumping into one another. They are completely out of sync! It's a disaster! They are in desperate need of a choreographer.

Has your life ever felt like the scene on that Broadway stage? When we give our lives over to anyone or anything other than God, they can resemble an unchoreographed dance—two steps forward, three steps back. Life can become a matter of just going through the motions, and we accomplish little, if anything, of value for ourselves or for others.

It's only through making God the Lord of our lives that we give meaning to our motions. When we seek God's direction through daily prayer and devotion, he becomes a choreographer for our lives.

As we seek for our actions to be more in touch with God's divine will, we begin to hear heaven's music, and our steps have an order and a direction that we have never experienced before. The psalmist says, "Teach me, O Lord, to follow every one of your principles. . . . Make me walk along the path of your commands, for that is where my happiness is found" (Psalm 119:33-35).

God doesn't reveal all of the good parts of the story in advance though. Oh, he tells us the glorious happy ending—everlasting life in heaven for those who accept his Son as Lord and Savior. But, like any good choreographer, he has the big picture in mind and expects us to trust him for the individual steps. He gives us just enough light and instruction for the step that is right in front of us!

You say you're not much of a dancer. That's OK. That's the thing about Christ. He transforms lives. Give him your sore, tired feet and your tangled-up steps, and let him make them into a fluid, grace-filled motion.

Trust the choreographer. He has just the right part picked out for you. In fact, no one else can dance your dance. Only you can dance the dance that God has for you! Let a passion for Christ reenergize you and infuse your days with purpose. With your heart committed to Jesus as the Lord of your dance, you will find new meaning in every move you make, serving him and his creation for the glory of God.

A Closer Connection

Who is your choreographer? What do you need to surrender to God so that his divine guidance can direct your steps?

A Challenge and . . .

I know, Lord, that a person's life is not his own. No one is able to plan his own course. So correct me, Lord, but please be gentle.
JEREMIAH 10:23-24

A Promise

Jesus said to the people, "I am the light of the world. If you follow me, you won't be stumbling through the darkness, because you will have the light that leads to life." JOHN 8:12

A Man after Your Own Heart

Written by Wayne Kirkpatrick and Billy Luz Sprague
Recorded by Gary Chapman
1996 Dove Inspirational Song of the Year

O God Father in heaven and earth
I call to You like deep calls to deep over water
Show me Your endless measure of grace
Let tender mercies shine once again
From Your holy face

Deep in my soul there's a craving
To please the One who has saved me
O God though I have fallen so far
You know that I'm still
A man after Your own heart

I am driven by rivers of pride
You are my rescue
The Maker and Keeper of my life
Lead me by the still waters again
Use me in spite of the prodigal child
That You know I am

CHORUS
Just as a deer runs to water
So does my soul to You Father
O God though I have wandered so far
You know that I'm still
A man after Your own heart
I'm still a man after Your own heart

A MAN AFTER YOUR OWN HEART

The Path of Obedience

Perhaps no other story in the Bible offers as much hope to our hopelessly wayward humanity as that of the Prodigal Son. At one time or another all of us have managed to get off course. It's all too easy to lose our way in a world that assigns so much value to things temporal—appearance, status, and power. With its message that there's a home to return to and forgiveness to be found, this story offers us the promise of a clean slate and a new beginning to those who repent and seek the comfort of the Father's welcoming arms.

Even King David, who was called a man after God's own heart, fell precipitously in his walk with the Lord, succumbing to temptation that ultimately led to adultery, betrayal, and murder. And he's not alone! In fact, time and time again in Scripture, God gives us examples of accomplishing his purposes through flawed, imperfect people. What encouragement that gives to us: God can work in our own less-than-perfect lives.

We must be careful, however, not to see this as an invitation to continue in our sin. Yes, sometimes we'll fall short of the mark. After all, our pride and ego can lead us astray. We can begin to trust in ourselves, especially when things are going our way, and develop an attitude of self-sufficiency that can lead us away from God. Yet we should be continually seeking after God's heart, continually seeking to be more like Christ.

In these chaotic and uncertain times, what does it mean for us to be people after God's own heart? Allow me to suggest a few things:

- It means that we seek to be obedient to God in all things (see 2 Corinthians 10:5).
- It means that we pray without ceasing, always alert and listening for God's will in our lives (see 1 Thessalonians 5:17; Deuteronomy 30:20).
- It means that we strive to set our minds on the ways of Christ (see Colossians 3:1-4).
- It means that we put the needs of others above our own (see Matthew 23:11).
- It means that we seek to be peacemakers (see Matthew 5:9).
- It means that we seek to reconcile ourselves to God and to help others to do the same (see 2 Corinthians 5:18-19).
- It means that we forgive (see Matthew 6:12; Luke 6:27).
- It means that we offer hope (see Isaiah 40:31).
- It means that we extend mercy and compassion (see Zechariah 7:9; Luke 6:36).
- It means that we are creative (see Genesis 1:27).
- It means that we celebrate the gift of life (Psalm 92:4).
- It means that we never give up on anybody (see Matthew 18:21-22).
- It means that we show respect for God's creation (see Psalm 104).
- It means that we stand for justice and speak out against oppression (see Isaiah 1:17).
- It means that we are in community with one another (see Hebrews 10:25).
- It means that we love our neighbors . . . and our enemies (see Luke 10:27; 6:27).

None of us can pretend to fathom the depths of God's own heart. These examples from Scripture give us a glimpse of the character of God's heart and some guidelines for our own behavior as we seek to be more in line with his holy character as we live our own lives.

Let us be faithful in prayer. And as "deep calls to deep" (Psalm 42:7, NIV), let us be faithful to be the people of God he longs for us to be—not judgmental, with a high and mighty, self-aggrandizing righteousness but a community of reclamation projects who have been welcomed home—sharing his message of love and redemption with a broken world.

A Closer Connection

What are some checks and balances you could build into your life to help you be more obedient to God? Pray for God's will to take precedence over your own. Examine the Scripture for other examples that illuminate the character of God's heart.

A Challenge and . . .

Love means doing what God has commanded us, and he has commanded us to love one another, just as you heard from the beginning. 2 JOHN 1:6

A Promise

Commit everything you do to the Lord. Trust him, and he will help you. He will make your innocence as clear as the dawn, and the justice of your cause will shine like the noonday sun.
PSALM 37:5-6

More Than Wonderful

Written by Lanny Wolfe
Recorded by Sandy Patty and Larnelle Harris
1984 Dove Song of the Year

He promised us that He would be a counselor
A mighty God and the Prince of Peace
He promised us that He would be a Father
And would love us with a love that would not cease
Well I tried Him and I found His promises are true
He's ev'rything He said that He would be
The finest words I know could not begin to tell
Just how much Jesus really means to me

CHORUS
For He's more wonderful than my mind can conceive
He's more wonderful than my heart can believe
He goes beyond my highest hopes and fondest dreams
He's ev'rything that my soul ever longed for
Everything He's promised and so much more
More than amazing
More than marvelous
More than miraculous could ever be
He's more than wonderful
That's what Jesus is to me

I stand amazed to think the King of glory
Would come to live within the heart of man
I marvel just to know He really loves me
When I think of who He is and who I am

MORE THAN WONDERFUL

In Your Own Words

Over the last one hundred years of popular song, lyricists have struggled with new and creative ways to express the inexpressible power of romantic love. They've made it sound like the weather ("You Are the Sunshine of My Life"), like food ("A Taste of Honey"), and even like disease ("I've Got You under My Skin"). Possessing a God-given talent for expression and a love of language, armed with thesauruses, rhyming dictionaries, quotation books, and other various tricks of the trade, lyricists have still fallen short of completely expressing the mystery of love. No matter to what lengths we go in an effort to explain love, let's face it, once you experience the real thing, the best song in the world isn't going to measure up.

If you've ever tried to describe how you feel about Jesus and found yourself completely tongue-tied, then maybe you can relate. You know you love him; you know you're grateful to him. But when you try to put it into words, it just sounds so . . . well, ordinary.

Let's roll out some adjectives. Is Jesus terrific? Sure, but that hardly seems an expansive enough word to describe him. *Terrific* is more like for, "Wow, that new Arnold Schwarzenegger movie is terrific!" How about *great?* No doubt about it. Jesus is great. He has done great things, but again it sounds too common for Jesus. "That's a great new dress you have on," seems a more appropriate use of the word.

For Christian songwriters, it's the ultimate challenge. How does one appropriately describe our indescribable Lord? Thankfully, God has given us the gift of music, which has a power to transcend all language boundaries as a way to communicate his glory. When combined with prayerfully considered lyrics created from a desire to be life giving, the songs can be inspirational and transformational, drawing us closer into the presence of Christ. But the greatest writer in the world would still admit that our best efforts at description pale in comparison to the actual person of Jesus.

The lyricist here has taken an obvious approach that captures the heart of the dilemma perfectly, overcoming it at the same time. Jesus is *more* than marvelous. Jesus is *more* than amazing. Jesus is *more* than miraculous.

So where does that leave us in talking about Jesus? If we're stuck with a language that seems to have no vocabulary large enough to encompass the wonderfulness of our Lord, there seems to be only one thing left to do. That is to talk about what he has done in our lives. What he has meant to us. How he has changed us. How he has taken the debris of our lives and reconciled us to himself, making something beautiful.

You may feel like your own story isn't remarkable enough to be worth telling. Maybe you don't feel as if you have a gift for expressing your feelings and experiences. Jesus doesn't need you to be Cole Porter or William Faulkner. He doesn't need you to be Steven Curtis Chapman or C. S. Lewis. He just needs you to be willing to be open and vulnerable, willing to share your own stories about the impact of Christian faith in your own life in an honest and direct way.

Your words may not sound like poetry to you. You may feel as if your testimony lacks pizzazz or charisma. But if the love of Christ has touched and transformed your life, then your story has all the power and beauty it needs to be meaningful for someone else. You never know how the uniqueness of your life experiences and faith journey will resonate for another. So don't criticize and edit yourself. Go ahead. Tell your story. Use ordinary words. Trust the One who is more than wonderful to make your story more than enough.

A Closer Connection

When was the last time you shared your faith story with someone? Pray for God to give you the words as you share about Christ from your heart this week.

A Challenge and . . .

I will live to tell what the Lord has done.   PSALM 118:17

A Promise

If anyone acknowledges me publicly here on earth, I will openly acknowledge that person before my Father in heaven.
MATTHEW 10:32

On My Knees

Written by David Mullen, Nicole C. Mullen, and Michael Ochs
Recorded by Jaci Velasquez
1997 Dove Song of the Year

There are the days when I feel
The best of me is ready to begin
Then there're days when I feel
I'm letting go and soaring on the wind
'Cause I've learned in laughter or in pain
How to survive

CHORUS
I get on my knees
I get on my knees
There I am before the love that changes me
See I don't know how
But there's pow'r
When I'm on my knees

I can be in a crowd
Or by myself almost anywhere
When I feel there's a need
To talk with God He is Emmanuel
When I close my eyes
No darkness there
There's only light

CHORUS

I don't know how
But there's power
In the blue skies
In the midnight
When I'm on my knees

ON MY KNEES
The Best Kind of Body Language

My wife tells a wonderful story about visiting her father in
Italy. Since he had been living there for several years, she
had made the reasonable, yet inaccurate, assumption that he
probably spoke a little of the language. Once overseas, she
accompanied her father to purchase some rubbing alcohol.
He walked up to the counter and began vigorously rubbing
his arm and saying "Vino! Vino!" repeatedly. Right away she
knew she was in trouble. Eventually, however, they were
able to communicate to the shopkeeper what they needed.

There are thousands of languages in the world, different
ways to communicate thoughts and feelings depending on
geographical location and ethnic background. If you've ever
traveled abroad, you probably know the helpless feeling
of being in a situation where you can't make your words
understood. But what about the other language that we all
speak, the one where we don't use any words at all?

It's called body language, and we all use it every day.
We communicate with a raised eyebrow, an upturned grin,
perhaps a shrug of the shoulders. We let people know
they're standing too close, that we're excited and happy to
see them, that we're frustrated or content, interested or
bored silly—all without saying a word. Even when we do
speak, we let our body language embellish our words and
shade their meaning.

What's even more interesting, however, is that our own body
language can communicate not only to others but to us as well.
When we stand up straight, we find ourselves suddenly feeling more confident and ready for action. Conversely, slouch-
ing can sap the very energy right out of us and make us feel
defeated even before we begin. When we smile, we can feel

anger and stress fade away. When we frown, we can feel ourselves filling up with dissatisfaction. Our minds listen to our bodies. Such is the case when we are on our knees.

What does being on our knees before God tell us even before we begin to pray?

It tells us that he is above us. When we are on our knees, there is no longer any pretense that we are in control. The very act of bowing to kneel puts us in a submissive stance that acknowledges that God is greater than we are. The apostle Paul writes, "When I think of the wisdom and scope of God's plan, I fall to my knees and pray to the Father, the Creator of everything in heaven and on earth" (Ephesians 3:14-15).

Praying on our knees changes the character of how we speak to God. We don't make many demands from our knees. On our knees we are more likely to bring our requests humbly before the Lord, more likely to acknowledge our own weakness and our need for repentance, more likely to acknowledge our thankfulness for his unmerited favor toward us.

Being on our knees even tells us something about the attitude we should take in our daily lives as we seek to be Christlike in our relationships with others.

"You can't look down on someone and look up at God at the same time," says Dr. Larry Keene. A day that starts with us on our knees is much more likely to be a day filled with humility and gratitude and therefore also a day on which we show the grace and mercy we've been shown.

After we've spent some time on our knees, we feel a little lighter, we have a little spring in our step. It's almost as if in kneeling before God we have allowed him to stoop down and lift our burdens off of our shoulders and bestow his blessing and his encouragement. In its nonconfrontationalness, kneeling is a position that invites him to be our Lord.

It's important to speak every day with our Lord, but there

are going to be times and places when it's impossible for us to get down on our knees, except in our hearts. But when it's not, let's often remember to bow reverently before the God who created us and offer our prayers.

A Closer Connection
What does it say about how much we value our prayer life if it's reduced to only hurried talks with God in the car or the shower? What kinds of changes can you make in your schedule to allow for more time on your knees with the Lord?

A Challenge and . . .
Because of this, God raised him up to the heights of heaven and gave him a name that is above every other name, so that at the name of Jesus every knee will bow, in heaven and on earth.
PHILIPPIANS 2:9-10

A Promise
The eyes of the Lord watch over those who do right, and his ears are open to their prayers.   1 PETER 3:12

Place in This World

Words and Music by Michael W. Smith, Wayne Kirkpatrick, and Amy Grant
Recorded by Michael W. Smith
1992 Dove Song of the Year

The wind is moving
But I am standing still
A life of pages
Waiting to be filled
A heart that's hopeful
A head that's full of dreams
But this becoming
Is harder than it seems

CHORUS
I'm looking for a reason
Roaming through the night to find
My place in this world
Not a lot to lean on
I need Your light to help me find
My place in this world

If there are millions
Down on their knees
Among the many
Can You still hear me?
Hear me asking
Where do I belong?
Is there a vision
That I can call my own?

PLACE IN THIS WORLD
Fulfillment the Jesus Way

There is a wonderful cartoon by B. Kliban. It has two frames. One shows a man sitting behind a desk at the office, busily pushing his pencil. The other shows another man sunning himself on a tropical beach. The caption reads "Wasted and Useful Lives," leaving the reader to decide which is which.

"What do you want to be when you grow up?" Even as children most of us instinctively set our sights high on careers that are exciting and adventurous. Presidents, astronauts, firefighters, ballplayers, rock musicians, and movie stars are some of the professions that make the list. It's harmless imagining. After all, doesn't little Johnny look cute in his fireman hat?

But very shortly thereafter it ceases to be cute. From a very early age children get the message that our society values those who are rich and/or famous. The pressure is on to be a doctor, a lawyer, or to pursue some other "worthwhile" profession. Emphasis is put on achievement. In the race to give our kids the winning edge, we push them into accelerated programs and label them "gifted." In the process we often forget to let them experience just being kids. The American divorce rate is over 40 percent, personal bankruptcies are at an all-time high, and people are burning out at an increasingly younger age. Why are we in such a hurry to make our children into "successful" adults?

Don't misunderstand. There is nothing inherently wrong with success. And education is always important at any age. But the question begs asking. Is our culture working? Is pushing hard to make good grades to get into a good college to get into a high paying profession to get into a large mortgage and a large car payment really worthwhile? Have our priorities gotten a little off course? Do we really own all the things we work so hard to acquire, or do they own us? At the end of the day, what is really important in our lives? When all is said and done, what kind of a difference are we going to make?

Deep down all of us want to live lives that make a difference. It's the way we're made. We long to find meaning and purpose for our days, and that all begins with turning to the One who gives us the days in the first place. Finding our place in this world is ultimately about finding God's will for our lives. As my friend Rick Goad says, "God's purpose *is* the purpose." When we look at our life through the lens of God's vision for us, our goals and desires begin to change. As we look at Christ's example of service to others, some of our confusion begins to ebb away. You've heard it said, "If you want to forget your troubles, then go help somebody who is worse off than you are."

In Mark 12 Jesus clearly said that no commandments are more important than to love God and to love our neighbor as ourself. Christ is making the point that in putting God and others first we will best fulfill our own desires. By serving others we are ironically putting ourselves on a path to our own personal fulfillment. Self*lessness* becomes the ultimate selfishness.

In the final analysis, it's not so much what you do but who you are while you're doing it that matters. Jesus doesn't care about status or wealth. He doesn't care about worldly standards of success. He doesn't even care about Dove awards. Whether you bag groceries or are a brain surgeon is beside the point. What he cares about is that we love each other.

Life can be hard sometimes. We all have our ups and downs. But as we struggle with the question of where we fit in the bigger picture, it is comforting to know that Jesus has given us a task to accomplish with and for others. When in doubt, love the way Christ loves.

A Closer Connection

Do you find your value in what you do or in who you are? What are some ways you could serve others in the daily routine you find yourself in right now?

A Challenge and . . .

Whoever wants to be a leader among you must be your servant.
MATTHEW 20:26

A Promise

What this world honors is an abomination in the sight of God.
LUKE 16:15

Redeemer

Written by Nicole Mullen
Recorded by Nicole Mullen
2001 Dove Song of the Year

Who taught the sun where to stand in the morning
And who told the ocean you can only come this far
And who showed the moon where to hide 'til evening
Whose words alone can catch a falling star

CHORUS
Well I know my Redeemer lives
I know my Redeemer lives
All of creation testifies
This life within me cries
I know my Redeemer lives

The very same God who spins things in orbit
Runs to the weary the worn and the weak
And the same gentle hands that hold me when I'm broken
They conquer death to bring me victory

Well I know my Redeemer lives
I know my Redeemer lives
Let all creation testify
Let this life within me cry
I know my Redeemer lives

He lives to take away my shame
And He lives forever I'll proclaim
That the payment for my sin
Was the precious life He gave
But now He's alive and there's an empty grave

REDEEMER

The Living Christ

It's a scene you've probably seen in several movies and television programs. A bereaved person kneels over a grave, sobbing with regret for words left unsaid. "I should have told you I was sorry," "I never even told you I loved you," and other similar phrases stream remorsefully from the one left behind.

Unfortunately it's all too true. We take for granted those who are closest to us, often keeping our deep affection locked away in our hearts, failing to share with others how important they really are to us. Then suddenly one day the opportunity to speak those words is gone forever. Or we let a disagreement with someone go unreconciled until it's too late to make amends.

We human beings are notorious procrastinators. It starts early, when we put off writing our big school report until the night before it's due. Then later on, as adults, we drive around for weeks with the car making a mysterious grinding sound when we know it's overdue for an unavoidable trip to the mechanic. Then there's that annual physical exam that we get around to every three or four years.

Death, however, will not be put off. And often it comes unexpectedly, rudely putting an end to unfinished conversations, robbing us of the option to set things right with others. Yet in his unending, unfailing mercy, God has provided us a way to know him and speak with him—the One who overcame even the normally unforgiving specter of death. Through the resurrection of Jesus and the miraculous indwelling of the Holy Spirit, we have the opportunity to be in relationship with the *living* Christ two thousand years after he walked the earth!

Thus, it's never too late to set things right with God. In

Jesus we have a redeemer who is always there for us. He always was, and he always will be. Whether we come to him at the age of nine or ninety, he's going to be there for us. The time is always right for the salvation of our souls.

This is particularly good news for those of us in mortal flesh. We are going to fall. We are going to sin. We are going to need to revisit the redeeming love of Christ on many occasions throughout our lives. And since our Redeemer lives yesterday, today, and tomorrow, we will always be able to count on him.

Of course, just because Jesus is always going to be there for us is no excuse to keep him waiting. Nowhere is the phrase "Don't put off until tomorrow what you can do today" more apt than describing our urgent need for a relationship with Christ. If you're already assured that you have that but have been harboring sins that you know you need to repent of, there's no time like the present.

As Christians we live as forgiven people. Yet we never want to take advantage of that gift of forgiveness by not repenting when we know we need to. The living Christ is our advocate before the Father. He has paid the price for our sins. It's important that in our relationship with him we leave nothing unsaid, no sin unacknowledged.

So look around you. Look at your friends and family and even at your enemies. What have you left unsaid? Bless somebody today by speaking your love to someone who might not know how much he or she means to you. Apologize to someone that you have carried a grudge against. Speak forgiveness to somebody who has wronged you. Do it in the name of your Redeemer, Jesus Christ.

While you're at it, speak from your heart to Jesus, too. He's alive, and he would love to hear from you today.

A Closer Connection

How have you compartmentalized Christ in the past? How does recognizing that Jesus is always with you lead you to change your behavior?

A Challenge and . . .

Now turn from your sins and turn to God, so you can be cleansed of your sins.   ACTS 3:19

A Promise

Then wonderful times of refreshment will come from the presence of the Lord, and he will send Jesus your Messiah to you again.   ACTS 3:20

Rise Again

Written by Dallas Holm
Recorded by Dallas Holm
1978 Dove Song of the Year

Go ahead
Drive the nails in My hands
Laugh at Me where you stand
Go ahead
And say it isn't Me
The day will come when you will see

CHORUS
'Cause I'll rise again
There's no pow'r on earth can tie Me down
Yes I'll rise again
Death can't keep Me in the ground

Go ahead
And mock My name
My love for you is still the same
Go ahead
And bury Me
But very soon I will be free

CHORUS

Go ahead
Say I'm dead and gone
But you will see that you were wrong
Go ahead
Try to hide the Son
But all will see that I'm the One

'Cause I'll rise again
Ain't no power on earth can keep Me back
Yes I'll come again
Come to take My people back

RISE AGAIN
An Unthinkable Gift

Have you ever given any thought to the excruciating pain
Jesus suffered at the Crucifixion? The following three para-
graphs are not meant to be gratuitously graphic. They are
simply meant to give the reader a fuller understanding of
what Jesus endured for us on the cross.

First, before Jesus went to the cross he was flogged (see
Mark 15:15). The Romans used a whip that was made up
of small pieces of bone and metal attached to a number of
leather strands. The flogging would have stripped the skin
from Jesus' back, exposing muscle and bone. Later a crown
of thorns was put on Jesus' head (Mark 15:17-18). The
Roman soldiers "beat Jesus on the head," driving the thorns
into the scalp, causing profuse bleeding.

Then after being flogged, tormented, and mocked all
night, Jesus was made to carry the crossbar of the cross to
Golgotha (see John 19); the crossbar is estimated to have
weighed between 80 and 110 pounds.

At Golgotha, the crucifixion began. Nails about 7 inches in
length and ⅜ of an inch in diameter were driven into Jesus'
wrists through to the cross, and his feet were also nailed.
Jesus suffered from a severe loss of blood.

"When the cross was erected upright, there was tremendous

strain put on the wrists, arms and shoulders, resulting in a dislocation of the shoulder and elbow joints." The position his body was hanging in made it impossible for him to take a full breath, and it was very difficult for him to exhale. Jesus' muscles cramped terribly, and painful spasms resulted from loss of blood, oxygen, and the fixed position of his body.

It's almost unbearable even to think about our beloved Savior enduring such unspeakable horror, isn't it? Why would our Lord go through something like this? The answer came three days later as Jesus had known all along that it would. "The Son of Man is going to be betrayed. He will be killed, but three days later he will rise from the dead," said Jesus in Mark 9:31.

Christ overcame death, not by resisting with force, but with conquering love. On the cross, "Jesus shouted out again, and he gave up his spirit" (Matthew 27:50).

He rose above the pain. He rose above the humiliation. He rose above death itself. But most important, he rose above *our sin*. In spite of the worst thing that we could do to him, he returned with the same unflagging message of peace, love, and forgiveness for all people. "There is forgiveness of sins for all who turn to me," he said in Luke 24:47 when he appeared to the disciples in Jerusalem. There it is. Love. Once and for all Jesus proved that love is more powerful than death.

"O death, where is your victory? . . . How we thank God, who gives us victory over sin and death through Jesus Christ our Lord!" exclaims Paul in 1 Corinthians 15:55-57. When we realize the magnitude of Christ's suffering on our behalf, it reframes for us our relationship with him. First of all, it calls us to an obedience of Jesus' commands, not borne of coercion but of a requited love. Second, it calls us to a willingness to make sacrifices on Jesus' behalf to further his dominion here on earth. We want to serve him. We want to share the kind

of self-sacrificing love Christ gave to us with the world. We
want our words and actions to point people to Jesus. We
realize that if Jesus could rise again after what he went
through, there's nothing in this world that we can't overcome in his name and through his love.

So, that's how Jesus was able to go through the crucifixion. For he knew that he would defeat death and open the
door to forgiveness for all of us.

A Closer Connection

Have you thanked Jesus recently for the sacrifice that he made
for you? What are some things that have left you feeling
defeated that you need to rise above in the name of Christ?

A Challenge and . . .

Turn from your sins and believe this Good News! MARK 1:15

A Promise

Be sure of this: I am with you always, even to the end of the age.
MATTHEW 28:20

Say the Name

Written by Margaret Becker and Charlie Peacock
Recorded by Margaret Becker
1995 Dove Nominee for Inspirational Recorded Song of the Year

A more sweeter sounding word
These lips have never said
A gentle Name so beautiful
My heart cannot forget
Just a whisper is enough
To set my soul at ease
Just thinking of this Name
Brings my heart to peace

CHORUS
Say the Name
Say the Name that soothes the soul
The Name of gentle healing
And peace immutable
I'll say the Name that has heard my cry
Has seen my tears and wiped them dry
From now until the end of time
I'll say the Name

May I never grow so strong
That my heart cannot be moved
May I never grow so weak
That I fear to speak the truth
I will say this holy Name
No matter who agrees
For no other name on earth
Means so much to me

SAY THE NAME

What's in a Name?

When a couple finds out they're pregnant, they begin feathering the nest. Excitedly, they begin working on the baby's room, painting and wallpapering. They begin collecting rocking chairs, stuffed animals, and baby clothes as they wait expectantly. One of the most important things they have to do to prepare for the baby is select a name. Hours and hours may be spent pouring over baby name books, making lists, and auditioning names on their tongues out loud. Each name suggests personality and character traits, though often different ones to different people. Winston may sound dignified, Garrett strong. Rosemary may sound refined, Daisy more playful. The challenge is to pick a name that will express all that the child will become and to do it *in advance!*

Perhaps you think you attach no importance to names. Ah, but you do. Pick for example your favorite NFL team. Can you imagine the Tennessee Titans, for example, being as fearsome if they were named the Tennessee Tulips?

America's sweetheart Doris Day might not have called to

mind such a sunny image if she had gone by her real name, Doris Von Kappelhoff. And would Cary Grant have seemed so irresistibly romantic as Archibald Leach? How differently would the successful Christian group Point of Grace have been perceived if *their* name had been Nine-Inch Nails?

Names matter.

Considering all of this makes the name of Jesus all the more remarkable. There is tremendous power in the name of Jesus. It is the kind of power that can bring gentle comfort in the most unbearable pain and the kind of power that can make the strongest evil turn and flee. It is the kind of power that is strong enough to oppose a mighty nation and compassionate enough to kneel and help a hurting child. It is a name that is sweet enough to embrace the deepest part of our souls with a tender love that is inexpressibly beautiful. It is a name terrible enough to frighten the darkest demon into submission with the blinding light of truth. It is a name that heals our spirits and overcomes all suffering. It is a name that speaks welcome to all who come humbly, seeking the face of God. It is a name that defeats all of our self-seeking arrogance and pride. Nothing can stand against the name of Jesus. Saying the name of Jesus can change your mood, your attitude—your very life.

Reflecting on the name of Jesus can bring a deep and abiding peace that surpasses anything this world has to offer. It is a peace that cannot be purchased with money, cannot be acquired through power, cannot be taken by force, cannot be obtained through sex, and cannot be conjured with drugs. It is divine, something from beyond this world. It is a window on heaven given us by God in the person of Christ indwelling our hearts through the Holy Spirit.

On this earth saying the name of Jesus is like a song! It is every great symphony heard. It is every glorious flower that has ever bloomed. It is every beautiful poem ever written. It is every mother that has ever held a child. It is life.

When you confess the name of Jesus, you are speaking your very own salvation. When you proclaim the name of Jesus, you are speaking peace to an aching world. The very name itself is transformational and transporting. It brings us to the foot of the cross. It brings us into the presence of God.

As Christians we are Christ's namesakes. As such may we never fail to honor his name, defend his name, and proclaim his name, especially in situations where it might make us feel uncomfortable. After all, how uncomfortable was he willing to be to save us?

Say the name. Pray the name. Jesus.

A Closer Connection

How often during the day does the name Jesus pass your lips? Be intentional about invoking the name of Jesus in all sorts of different situations in the coming week, and see what kind of difference it makes.

A Challenge and . . .

There is salvation in no one else! There is no other name in all of heaven for people to call on to save them. ACTS 4:12

A Promise

Yes, ask anything in my name, and I will do it! JOHN 14:14

Shine

Written by Peter Furler and Steve Taylor
Recorded by The Newsboys
1996 Dove Song of the Year

Dull as dirt
You can't assert the kind of light
That might persuade a strict dictator to retire
Fire the army
Teach the poor origami
The truth is in
The proof is when
You hear your heart start asking
What's my motivation
And try as you may there isn't a way
To explain the kind of change
That would make an Eskimo renounce fur
That would make a vegetarian barbecue hamster
Unless you trace this about-face to a certain sign

CHORUS
Shine
Make 'em wonder what you've got
Make 'em wish that they were not
On the outside lookin' bored
Shine
Let it shine before all men
Let 'em see good works and then
Let 'em glorify the Lord

Out of the shaker and onto the plate
It isn't karma it sure ain't fate
That would make a Deadhead sell his van
That would make a schizophrenic turn in his crayons
Oprah freaks and science seeks a rationale

202

That shall excuse this strange behavior
When you let it shine you will inspire
The kind of entire turnaround
That would make a bouncer take ballet
Even bouncers who aren't happy
But out of the glare
With nowhere to turn
You ain't gonna learn it on "What's My Line"

SHINE

Making a Spectacle

Have you ever seen a Hollywood premiere? In the street in front of the theater large searchlights are positioned to shoot their beams upward, crisscrossing the sky. A red carpet runs from the street to the theater entrance. The celebrities step from their limousines decked out in dazzling finery—from designer gowns and strings of diamonds to tuxedos. The cameras of the paparazzi flash relentlessly, and the crowds, restrained by ropes and security guards, scream out, trying to grab the attention of their favorite movie stars as they pass by. You'd think something really incredible was happening! But actually it's just another movie. There have been thousands and thousands of them.

America is really good at spectacle. We can make the most mundane events into mega-events in the blink of an eye. Release ten thousand balloons, have a rock star sing the national anthem, and a guy jump out of an airplane, and voila!—it's not just a baseball game anymore. I've been to car lot openings that looked like a small country celebrating its first Independence Day. But, as the old Wendy's commercial used to say, "Where's the beef?"

Christians have such a great reason to make a spectacle. We have the best news anybody has ever had to share. Churches needn't try to compete with a world that is committed to appearances. As a matter of fact there's a dangerous pitfall lurking there. In sharing the gospel we never want to set the precedent of putting style before substance. However, if we're passionate about our faith, we need to do more than simply reserve our celebrating to decorating the house at Christmastime and getting dressed up on Easter. We need to be willing to make a spectacle out of *ourselves* for the sake of the gospel.

When we have the love of Christ living in our hearts, a change has come over us.

It's a change that the whole world should *see*. "Don't hide your light under a basket!" Jesus says. "Instead, put it on a stand and let it shine for all" (Matthew 5:15).

In his novel of the emerging church, *Paul*, biblical scholar Walter Wangerin Jr. describes the first century apostle as "the drum, the trumpet, and the shepherd's pipe." When he spoke, "words burst from his mouth like flocks of birds, and the faith of the man was a high wind at the hearts of the people." This was someone who was willing to make a spectacle of himself for the cause of Christ. Consider Paul's words in Philippians 4:4: "Always be full of joy in the Lord. I say it again—rejoice!" This is somebody who knows how to shine.

Not all of us are gifted public speakers or preachers like the apostle Paul. However, God has given each of us special gifts that we can use to bring glory to his kingdom and encourage people in faith.

It's one thing to draw attention to ourselves for our own gain. It's another thing entirely to draw attention to ourselves in order that we may direct others toward the One in whom we place our hope. When we're plugged into God, it's *his* light we want people to see. Let's not be so timid that we appear ashamed of the gospel we profess, hiding our lamp under a basket. Instead, may we boldly and joyfully proclaim the gospel, each in our own way—whether in song, in acts of loving-kindness, in the written word, or in the words we speak—until the unmistakable light of Christ touches everyone we meet.

So go on, make a spectacle of yourself! May it be said of you—*that* is someone who knows how to shine.

A Closer Connection

How do you think others would describe the way you share your faith? What are some of the ways you are letting your light "shine for all"?

A Challenge and . . .

Let your good deeds shine out for all to see, so that everyone will praise your heavenly Father.   MATTHEW 5:16

A Promise

The Lord is my light and my salvation.   PSALM 27:1

Shout to the Lord

Words and Music by Darlene Zschech
Recorded by the Hillsongs Worship Team
1998 Dove Nominee for Song of the Year

My Jesus
My Savior
Lord there is none like You
All of my days
I want to praise
The wonders of Your mighty love
My comfort
My shelter
Tower of refuge and strength
Let every breath all that I am
Never cease to worship You

CHORUS
Shout to the Lord
All the earth let us sing
Power and majesty praise to the King
Mountains bow down and the seas will roar
At the sound of Your name
I sing for joy
At the works of Your hands
Forever I'll love You
Forever I'll stand
Nothing compares to the promise I have in You

SHOUT TO THE LORD
Lives That Shout!

When a forty-two-year-old seamstress, civil rights worker, and devout Christian refused to give up her seat on a Montgomery, Alabama, bus in 1955, she didn't have to raise her voice. Yet Rosa Parks's act of civil disobedience against the legally sanctioned discrimination of her day was a shout! It was a clarion call that awakened an entire nation and put in motion the events that eventually led to the Civil Rights Act of 1964 and an end to lawful segregation in the United States.

When a thirty-eight-year-old nun and teacher left the convent to pursue a life of service to the underprivileged of India, there was no earthly acclaim, no publicity machine to stir up a fuss. But after nearly fifty years of providing medical care, warm meals, and spiritual nurture to thousands of discarded and destitute people halfway around the world, Mother Teresa became a household name in America. Her quiet life of service did the shouting for her.

When an eighteen-year-old North Carolina farm boy and Fuller brush salesman found himself talking to his customers about Christ more than about the brushes he was supposed to be selling, he couldn't have known that it was the beginning of a ministry that would last for more than six decades. But Billy Graham started talking about the love of Jesus and never stopped. Millions of people have given their hearts to Christ in Billy Graham crusades.

We scream and shout ourselves silly at sporting events. You'd think the fate of the world hung in the balance when the Super Bowl rolls around. But without looking it up, quick, name the winner of the 1992 Super Bowl. Unless your team won that year, you probably don't remember. But there's no doubt that you know who Rosa Parks, Mother Teresa, and

Billy Graham are. That's because their lives and actions were something worth shouting about. Something eternal.

While the growing trend in contemporary praise and worship shows that we are willing to be more vocal about God inside our church walls, we must always ask ourselves if we are keeping too much of that enthusiasm to ourselves instead of sharing it with the world. And it's not just about evangelism. What we *do* matters just as much and maybe more than what we say. Ralph Waldo Emerson said, "I can't hear what you're saying because your life is talking so loudly."

We need to be careful that what we *shout* about shows up in our behavior. If we are wearing the name of Christ and talking about forgiveness of sins, then we need to make sure we are being forgiving in our personal lives. If we're championing Jesus as the Prince of Peace, then we need to be sure that we're working to be peacemakers in our families and at our workplaces. Our praise and worship needs to permeate our thinking so thoroughly that we can't help but act in ways that are in concert with Jesus. The resulting compassion and mercy shown will speak so loudly that people will be drawn to listen and anxious to know what motivates us.

In Psalm 147:1 we are exhorted, "Praise the Lord! How good it is to sing praises to our God! How delightful and how right!" It's important to sing our praises to God. We can't all be a Rosa Parks, a Mother Teresa, or a Billy Graham, but we can live so that our passion and our worship enter the fabric of our daily lives—so that *every* act is an act of worship. Only then will our lives truly shout to the Lord!

A Closer Connection
What are some different ways you can worship God every day of the week? How is your life shouting, "Jesus Christ is my Lord and Savior"?

A Challenge and . . .

Those who say they live in God should live their lives as Christ did.   1 JOHN 2:6

A Promise

Praise the Lord, all you nations. Praise him, all you people of the earth. For he loves us with unfailing love; the faithfulness of the Lord endures forever. Praise the Lord!   PSALM 117

Sometimes He Calms the Storm

Written by Kevin Stokes and Tony Wood
Recorded by Scott Krippayne
1997 Dove Nominee for Inspirational Song of the Year

All who sail the sea of faith
Find out before too long
How quickly blue skies can grow dark
And gentle winds grow strong
Suddenly fear is like white water
Pounding on the soul
Still we sail on knowing
That our Lord is in control

CHORUS
Sometimes He calms the storm
With a whispered peace be still
He can settle any sea
But it doesn't mean He will
Sometimes He holds us close
And lets the wind and waves go wild
Sometimes He calms the storm
And other times He calms His child

He has a reason for each trial
That we pass through in life
And though we're shaken
We cannot be pulled apart from Christ
No matter how the driving rain beats down
On those who hold to faith
A heart of trust will always
Be a quiet peaceful place

SOMETIMES HE CALMS
THE STORM
All the Lifeboat We Need

There was a woman at a church I once attended who had four children. She also had an elderly friend living in one of her bedrooms. With her husband, that made a family of seven people. The family also had a dog, two cats, a hamster, and an iguana. At the time my wife and I had only one child. Whenever we would visit this home or see this woman at church, we would be struck by her total sense of peace. No matter what kind of chaos orbited around her, she would always seem to be serene. One day when her oldest son was doing gymnastics on the living-room sofa, I commented on her calmness and asked her how she remained so unruffled by the frenzy of her large family. "Oh, this is nothing," she replied. "I had *nine* brothers and sisters!"

This calm mother had been taught from an early age that the most important ingredient for a happy family was love. Just as it was love of family that made her noisy home an oasis for our friend, so it is that love of God can bring peace to us in the disquieting times of our lives.

In Psalm 46:10 God commands us, "Be silent, and know that I am God!" But that requires some discipline. It's one thing to find that peace when things are going your way. It's another thing entirely when the world is falling down around you.

I have known people who think of God as some sort of spiritual Santa Claus. They pray for the things they want, and then their faith wavers if they don't get their way. When any kind of calamity strikes, they are in danger of losing their faith completely. It would be great if accepting Christ meant that nothing bad would ever happen to us again. But like the old song says, "I never promised you a rose garden." If we are blessed to live long enough, calamity

211

will strike us *all*, Christian and non-Christian alike. "For he gives his sunlight to both the evil and the good, and he sends rain on the just and on the unjust, too" (Matthew 5:45).

Will there be times when Christ calms the stormy seas in your life? Absolutely. I believe that any person who believes in Jesus and has a regular, passionate prayer life will experience the peace that only Christ can give.

However, there will be other times when the storm is going to blow and keep right on blowing. Loved ones are going to pass away, and the grief will linger. Physical illness is going to interrupt your plans and demand your attention. You may lose a job and face prolonged uncertainty about your income. Life is full of harrowing challenges. But it all comes back to the love of God. No matter how our boat may rock, it will never be capsized as long as we carry the love of Christ in our hearts. If we have confidence in that love and place our trust in the One who gives it to us, then we have all the lifeboat we need in any squall.

As Paul writes in Romans 8:38-39, "Our fears for today, our worries about tomorrow, and even the powers of hell can't keep God's love away. Whether we are high above the sky or in the deepest ocean, nothing in all creation will ever be able to separate us from the love of God that is revealed in Christ Jesus our Lord."

Yes, sometimes he calms the storm. But even when he doesn't—in chaos, want, sickness, and confusion—the love of God that surpasses all of our understanding is *always* present with us.

A Closer Connection
What do you do at the first sign of trouble? When difficulties come, are there some favorite Scriptures that you turn to that reassure you of God's continuing care for you?

A Challenge and . . .

O my people, trust in him at all times. Pour out your heart to him, for God is our refuge. PSALM 62:8

A Promise

I am leaving you with a gift—peace of mind and heart. And the peace I give isn't like the peace the world gives. So don't be troubled or afraid. JOHN 14:27

Sometimes Miracles Hide

Words and Music by Bruce Carroll and C. Aaron Wilburn
Recorded by Bruce Carroll
1992 Country Recorded Song of the Year

They were so excited it was coming to be
Two people so in love . . . now soon there would be three
For many years they'd planned it
Now it would soon be true
She was picking out the pink clothes
He was looking at the blue

The call came unexpected
The doctor had bad news
Some tests came back and things weren't right
He said, "You're going to have to choose
I'll wait a week for your decision"
Then the words cut like a knife:
"I'm sure everyone will understand
If you want to end its life"

Though they were badly shaken
They just had no choice
They knew God creates no accidents
And they were sure they heard His voice saying

CHORUS
Sometimes miracles hide
God will wrap some blessings in disguise
You may have to wait this lifetime
To see the reasons with your eyes
'Cause sometimes miracles hide

It seemed before they knew it
The appointed day arrived
With eager apprehension

They could barely hold inside
The first time they laid eyes on her
Confirmed the doctor's fears
But they held on to God's promises
'Cause they were sure they both could hear

CHORUS

Though she was not like the other girls
They thought she was the best
And through all the years of struggle
Neither whispered one regret
On the first day that she started school
And took her first bus ride
They remembered the words that God had spoke
And they both broke down and cried

See to them it did not matter
Why some things in life take place
They just knew the joy they felt
When they looked into her face
They learned

Sometimes miracles hide
They said, "God has wrapped our blessing in disguise
We may have to wait this lifetime
To see the reasons with our eyes
But we know sometimes miracles hide"

SOMETIMES MIRACLES HIDE
When You Can't See the Answer

Who of us has not experienced the devastating loss of a job or a broken relationship only to later find our situation not only healed but greatly improved by something new and better that God had in mind for us?

So often it seems that we get to the end of our rope. We can't see an answer or find a solution on our own to the problem that we are facing. But that's *exactly* when God does his best work—when we are at the *end* of ourselves. God specializes in surprises.

The lyrics to this song press a painful replay button in my memory. My wife and I had gone in for what we thought would be a routine ultrasound. This was our second pregnancy, so we thought we knew exactly what to expect. Then the technician spoke the chilling words, "I hate to be the one to tell you this."

In those few seconds our world came crashing down, and we knew our lives would never be the same again. My wife was carrying a baby with spina bifida.

We were quickly ushered into a meeting with a doctor we had never met before, a specialist on the disorder. He immediately urged us to abort. "You are going to have a very sick child. The odds are that he will never walk. He'll probably be paralyzed from the waist down."

But sometimes miracles hide. What started as a nightmare has become a fountain of blessing.

Not only does our son walk. He *runs*. He plays baseball and basketball. Ask him about himself, and he'll tell you he's an athlete and a musician. That's right. He plays the *drums*. In fact, quite contrary to being paralyzed, he is never still. Sometimes miracles hide.

But our son is not without his medical issues. What's more, for many of the other families that we meet walking along this road, the physical outcomes for their children's conditions are not as happy. Where are the miracles found then?

I can only answer from our experience.

We have witnessed the miracle of hundreds of people, both friends and strangers, being drawn into closer relationship with God through their daily fervent prayer for our child.

We have experienced the miracle of eyes opened and career paths changed as parents of a special-needs child. We've discovered new depths of compassion within our hearts through the lessons in our own lives.

We have experienced the unexpected bittersweet joy and extraordinary closeness as a family that comes from meeting the daily challenges of our son's condition.

"Special needs kids are compensated in the spirit," said Larry Keene, pastor for thirty years at Church in the Valley in Van Nuys, California, when we shared the diagnosis with him. In the light of our son's life we have grown to see the truth of those words.

Sometimes miracles hide.

Whatever serious difficulties you are facing right now— physical, emotional, spiritual, financial—you are not alone. No matter what you're going through, God is working in your circumstances to create a blessing. Hold on to hope. Hold on to faith. Remember the miraculous life of Jesus. God is in the miracle business.

Sometimes miracles hide.

A Closer Connection

What are some of the problems in your life or in the lives of others for which you cannot see an answer? When you feel

discouraged, do you give in to despair or pray expectantly
and trust in God?

A Challenge and . . .

*O my people, trust in him at all times. Pour out your heart to
him, for God is our refuge.*   Psalm 62:8

A Promise

*We know that God causes everything to work together for the
good of those who love God and are called according to his
purpose for them.*   Romans 8:28

Step by Step

Written by Beaker
Recorded by Rich Mullins
1993 Dove Nominee for Song of the Year

Oh God You are my God
And I will ever praise You
Oh God You are my God
And I will ever praise You
I will seek You in the morning
And I will learn to walk in Your ways
And step by step You'll lead me
And I will follow You all of my days

STEP BY STEP

A Light for Our Path

Like normal youngsters my kids would rather be hanging out
with friends or playing on the weekend than digging in for
another week of school and homework. It was against that back-
drop that I was recently talking with my teenage daughter and
her younger brother, giving them the "don't wish your life away"
lecture. My daughter then dramatically replied, "You only have
one chance to live this second," and then after waiting a beat
exclaimed breathlessly, "It's gone! It's gone! It's gone!"

As funny as the enactment of her observation was, it was
also startling to me for its demonstration of the truth. We
won't be getting any second chances with our seconds. Once
lived, they *are* gone. So how do we make the best use of this
precious commodity called time?

Well, we can start by being fully present, by living the
moment we're in—one step at a time. We human beings sure
are good at getting ahead of ourselves.

We waste countless hours of our lives worrying about
things, the majority of which never even happen. "How are
we going to pay this doctor's bill?" Then insurance covers it.
"What will we do if it rains on the day of Joni's birthday
picnic?" Then the sun shines. We worry about whether we'll
have enough money to pay for college when our kids are still
in the cradle, about what we're going to do in retirement
when we're still batting cleanup on the church softball team.
In short, we just worry. Jesus knew that about us. "Can all
your worries add a single moment to your life? Of course
not!" Christ asks and answers in Luke 12:25. That's also the
reason he said, "Don't worry about tomorrow, for tomorrow
will bring its own worries" (Matthew 6:34).

When I get ahead of myself, my dear friend Rick Altizer

always says. "God has not given you tomorrow. It belongs to him. He has only given you this moment." In Psalm 119:105 the psalmist says, "Your word is a lamp for my feet and a light for my path." Notice he didn't say a halogen headlight that illuminates the next mile and a half. God's word is a lamp for our feet as we walk the path that is right before us, for the very next step. If we take that one step in faith, even if it's a little wobbly, God will be there to shine his light and guide the way.

Sometimes it may even feel like you've lifted your leg to take that next step and there's no ground where your foot is about to land. But for those who place their trust in the Lord he will always set them on terra firma. As David writes in Psalm 40:2, "He lifted me out of the pit of despair, out of the mud and the mire. He set my feet on solid ground and steadied me as I walked along."

It all begins with where we focus our attention. If we rise in the morning with our eyes focused on God, if we seek to follow his will and obey his commandments, if we place our trust in Christ, then our path can't help but be illuminated.

The time we are given is a gift from God. As Rich Mullins's untimely death reminds us, we have no idea how much of it we're going to get. It's given in increments. Whether we think of time as days, hours, minutes, or seconds doesn't really matter. What matters is that we understand that no matter how we measure it, the gift of time is nonreturnable, nonrelivable. So this next step is the important one. It's the only one we're certain we get to take. Given that, let's live our lives step-by-step in communion with Jesus Christ so that our lives may show forth his praise today.

A Closer Connection

What have been the results when you have tried to outrun God, taking the second step before he has revealed the first?

When you start to worry about the future, what could you do instead?

A Challenge and . . .

Stay on the path that the Lord your God has commanded you to follow. Deuteronomy 5:33

A Promise

The Lord, your Redeemer, the Holy One of Israel, says: I am the Lord your God, who teaches you what is good and leads you along the paths you should follow. Isaiah 48:17

Thank You

Written by Ray Boltz
Recorded by Ray Boltz
1990 Dove Song of the Year

I dreamed I went to heaven
You were there with me
We walked upon the streets of gold
Beside the crystal sea
We heard the angels singing
And someone called your name
You turned and saw this young man
He was smiling as he came
And he said friend you may not know me now
Then he said but wait
You used to teach my Sunday school
When I was only eight
And ev'ry week you would say a prayer
Before the class would start
And one day when you said that prayer
I asked Jesus in my heart

CHORUS
Thank you for giving to the Lord
I am a life that was changed
Thank you for giving to the Lord
I am so glad you gave

Then another man stood before you
He said remember the time
A missionary came to your church
His pictures made you cry
You didn't have much money
But you gave it anyway
Jesus took the gift you gave
That's why I'm here today

CHORUS

One by one they came
Far as the eye could see
Each life somehow touched by your generosity
Little things that you had done
Sacrifices made
Unnoticed on the earth
In heaven now proclaimed
I know up in heaven
You're not supposed to cry
But I am almost sure
There were tears in your eyes
As Jesus took your hand
You stood before the Lord
He said My child look around you.
For great is your reward

THANK YOU
A Pebble in a Pond

Have you ever thrown a pebble into a pond? Concentric circles ring out from the point where the stone enters the water. If you stand and watch long enough, eventually you will be able to see the water gently lapping against the shore around the entire circumference of the pond. That one small action—tossing a pebble—has affected *all* the surface water in the pond!

The tiniest action we take can have very large repercussions. I'm reminded of a story I heard on the news a few years ago. When a patron at a drive-through coffee house was charged for his drink, he said, "Here's a few extra dollars to pay for the person behind me." It was reported that the gift was passed on to the next *nineteen* cars! A pebble in a pond.

In our hectic, modern lives it's often easy to overlook the people right in front of us. I've seen people at the post office or grocery store talking on their cell phones complete an entire transaction without ever actually speaking to the person behind the counter. As Christians we must never allow ourselves to buy into the idea that some encounters are insignificant. In Colossians 3:17 Paul says, "Whatever you do or say, let it be as a representative of the Lord Jesus." Every interaction, no matter how small, is a chance to share the love of Christ with another person. To treat it any other way is to devalue the individual as well as the opportunity that God has provided.

We've all had the experience of encountering a particularly pleasant salesclerk who was so genuinely helpful and friendly that we walked away from the store feeling better than we did when we walked in. If we wear the love of Christ as we go about the daily activities of our lives, we can similarly touch and brighten the day of every person with whom we come in contact. In turn, they are likely to pass that goodwill on to others they meet. A pebble in a pond.

Some pebbles are larger than others. Likely as not, there's at least one person who has been an important mentor in your life. Perhaps it was a Sunday school teacher, a coach, or a tutor— maybe an older sibling, a grandparent, or a neighbor. This person may have taught you invaluable lessons, helped define your morality, or given you important spiritual guidance. Think about it—someone even introduced you to Jesus Christ! That person changed your life for the better—forever! The pebble he or she tossed was more like a boulder in a birdbath!

Your life is going to affect others. There's no doubt about it. The only question is whether it will be for better or for worse. Will people walk away from you wanting to know more about Jesus because of the light they have seen in you?

Or will they walk away from you feeling judged, rejected, or ignored, turning away from Jesus in the process and blaming him for your behavior?

We who wear the name Christian can't go blithely through life assuming that since we're saved we've got it made and nothing we do after that matters much. *Everything* we do as Christians matters because it reflects upon Christ. Everything we do is another pebble in the pond.

Let's live our lives so that others will be thankful that they have known us. Let's live our lives so that the ripples we create with our lives are ripples of compassion, peace, joy, and love. Let's live our lives so that when we reach the finish line, Jesus will meet us there to say, "Well done, my good and faithful servant."

A Closer Connection

If someone had been watching you during the last week and judging Christianity based on your behavior, what would they have concluded about Jesus? What are some ways you could be a blessing to others in ordinary, everyday situations?

A Challenge and . . .

Don't hide your light under a basket! Instead, put it on a stand and let it shine for all. In the same way, let your good deeds shine out for all to see, so that everyone will praise your heavenly Father. MATTHEW 5:15-16

A Promise

No one has ever seen God. But if we love each other, God lives in us, and his love has been brought to full expression through us. I JOHN 4:12

Watercolour Ponies

Written by Wayne Watson
Recorded by Wayne Watson
From the 1988 Dove Pop/Contemporary Album of the Year

There are watercolour ponies
On my refrigerator door
And the shape of something I don't really recognize
Brushed with careful little fingers
And put proudly on display
A reminder to us all of how time flies
Seems an endless mound of laundry
And a stairway laced with toys
Gives a blow by blow reminder of the war
That we fight for their well-being
For their greater understandin'
To impart a holy rev'rence for the Lord

CHORUS
But baby what will we do
When it comes back to me and you
They look a little less like little boys ev'ry day
Oh the pleasure of watchin' the children growin'
Is mixed with a bitter cup
Of knowin' the watercolour ponies
Will one day ride away

And the vision can get so narrow
As you view through your tiny world
And little victories can go by with no applause
But in the greater evaluation
As they fly from your nest of love
May they mount up with wings as eagles for His cause

WATERCOLOUR PONIES
Raising Christian Kids

Can you remember the feeling you used to have when it was the first day of summer vacation? Three whole months! Those ninety days of freedom stretched out so far before you that you couldn't even conceive of September.

Of course now, as the parent, my view is much different. "Is it time to get everybody up for the 7:00 A.M. school bus already? It seems like they just got out for summer break two weeks ago!"

As a parent I have encountered some conflicting feelings about the passage of time. When my daughter was born, I adored watching her grow through the different stages of baby- and toddlerhood. "This is the best!" I would say. "I wish I could stop time so she could always stay the way she is right now." Then six weeks later I'd be saying, "No, *this* is the best!" Each stage was so exciting. A few weeks ago the thirteen-year-old version of my Stephanie walked through the room. "Who is that?" I asked my wife. "She didn't live here yesterday."

To say that kids are only little for a short while is to seriously understate the case. It's more like a heartbeat!

Since we have our children under our roof for such a limited time, it's imperative that we be very intentional in teaching them about God. There are three things we need to be aware of in trying to provide a good environment for our kids' spiritual growth. By the way, those of you who aren't parents—take note. An aunt, uncle, older cousin, or friend of the family can be an important spiritual mentor.

First of all, the most important thing is making time. In our hectic, overscheduled lives sometimes time is the hardest thing to give your kids—the undivided attention kind of time. I actually saw a dad bring his son to the ice-cream store, order the ice cream, sit and eat it, and then leave *without ever getting off his cell phone!* That's not the kind of time I mean. If we want our kids to listen to us, first we have to show them that we're truly interested in *them*. When we talk about the importance of a relationship with Jesus, they will be much more likely to be receptive if they have experienced a relationship with us. Time is how we show our kids we love them. Not stuff. Not money. Time.

After time, the next most important thing is to walk the talk. Mom, don't tell your daughter not to talk behind someone's back and then let her overhear you gossiping on the phone. Dad, don't tell your son that God wants him to honor his father and mother and then let him hear you speak disrespectfully to his mom. I wish I had a dollar for every time my son has copied my poor behavior within thirty seconds of a slip up. Be vigilant. Your children are watching, and they are far more likely to do as you do than as you say.

Finally, don't forget to pray for and with your kids. Pray for their schooling, pray for their spiritual lives, pray for their future spouse. Let them see you praying. If they see that prayer is important to you, it will be important to them.

Teach them how to pray, and give them opportunities to do it. Pray with them before they leave the house, at bedtime, and anytime they have an important dance recital, ballgame, or a big test coming up.

Parenting is the toughest job in the world. A soul has been entrusted to your care. What an awesome responsibility. Ironically, from the very moment your beloved children are born you are teaching them how to leave you. You just want to make sure that when they do, they will take a love for Jesus with them.

So go ahead. Turn your refrigerator into an art gallery. Cherish the present.

And cherish your kids enough to give them a foundation of faith that will last a lifetime.

A Closer Connection

How much time do you spend talking with your kids about Jesus? What time of the day or week can you intentionally designate as time for family Bible reading or other spiritually based family activities?

A Challenge and . . .

You must love the Lord your God with all your heart, all your soul, and all your strength. And you must commit yourselves wholeheartedly to these commands I am giving you today. Repeat them again and again to your children. Talk about them when you are at home and when you are away on a journey, when you are lying down and when you are getting up again.
DEUTERONOMY 6:5-7

A Promise

Teach your children to choose the right path, and when they are older, they will remain upon it.   PROVERBS 22:6

We Fall Down

Words and Music by Kyle Matthews
Recorded by Donnie McClurkin
2001 Dove Gospel Song of the Year

Cursing ev'ry step of the way, he bore a heavy load
To the market ten miles away
The journey took its toll
And ev'ry day he passed
A monastery's high cathedral walls
And it made his life seem meaningless and small

And he wondered how it would be
To live in such a place
To be warm well-fed and at peace
To shut the world away
So when he saw a priest
Who walked for once beyond the iron gate
He said tell me of your life inside that place
And the priest replied

CHORUS
We fall down
We get up
We fall down
We get up
We fall down
We get up
And the saints are just the sinners who fall down
And get up

Disappointment followed him home
He'd hoped for so much more
But he saw himself in a light
He had never seen before
'Cause if the priest who fell

Could find the grace of God to be enough
Then there must be some hope for the rest of us
Then there must be hope for the rest of us
'Cause

WE FALL DOWN
Why We Need Grace

"Those who become Christians become new persons. They are not the same anymore, for the old life is gone. A new life has begun!"

With this encouraging statement in 2 Corinthians 5:17, the apostle Paul lays the groundwork for new Christians to leave their sinful ways behind. Only that's not the whole story. Christians, even the most devout among us, are still sinners. Oh, we sin a lot *less*, hopefully, than we did before we came to know Christ. But we're still human. To sin, translated literally, means to miss the mark. Every person living in the flesh, no matter how God-focused he endeavors to be, will occasionally miss the mark. Making mistakes ought to be on that list of life's guarantees along with death and taxes. That's why we need grace, because we fall down.

Although we may not be murderers or bank robbers, that doesn't get us off the hook. Gossiping behind a friend's back, enjoying a little off-color joke around the watercooler, letting loose with a curse word in a moment of anger, sneaking home a few office supplies, mentally undressing an NFL cheerleader—take your pick. Sin is sin. And we all do it.

It's not that our hearts aren't in the right place. In fact, as Christians our hearts have been made new. Our minds have been changed. In Christ we have a new moral compass. We see and think about things differently, looking through the lens of our Christian faith. That changes the way we behave—*most* of the time. But once in a while we slip up. We fall down. After all, we're still in the flesh.

Another of Paul's statements in Romans 7:15 accurately depicts the struggle of Christians to avoid sin: "I don't understand myself at all, for I really want to do what is right, but I don't do it. Instead, I do the very thing I hate." In verse 19 he says, "When I want to do good, I don't. And when I try not to do wrong, I do it anyway."

If Paul, who underwent the most dramatic conversion in all of the New Testament, couldn't keep from sinning now and then, certainly we should not expect to be any different. Clearly, being a new person in Christ does not completely remove us from the power of sin. That's why we need grace.

Perhaps you are saying to yourself, "But it's different with me.

I *really* fell. How can God possibly forgive me for *this?*"

Are you an alcoholic who has fallen off the wagon? Christ will forgive you. You can get back up. Have you committed adultery or run out on your wife and kids? Christ will forgive you. You can get back up. Have you lied to someone, stolen from someone, said hateful things about someone? Christ will forgive you. You can get back up.

The Scripture says, "For all have sinned; all fall short of God's glorious standard" (Romans 3:23). You are not the only one who has fallen. *Everyone* who has ever set foot on the earth has fallen, except for Christ.

All of the saints were sinners. The disciples were sinners. The apostle Paul was a sinner. St. Augustine was a sinner. Martin Luther King Jr. was a sinner. Mother Teresa was a sinner. What excellent company we are in! The saints are just the sinners who fall down and get up to seek and to serve Christ for another day.

That's why we need grace.

There's no shame in having fallen. If we honestly desire redemption and confess our sins to Jesus, he will help us to get back up and overcome our failures. This is by no means, however, an invitation to keep sinning deliberately. Instead, it is the realization that only in trying to go it alone can we achieve the ultimate failure—trusting in ourselves more than Christ.

A Closer Connection

What are some areas where you've been unforgiving of yourself? Who are the people in your life you need to forgive, as God has forgiven you?

A Challenge and . . .

We are made right in God's sight when we trust in Jesus Christ to take away our sins.   ROMANS 3:22

A Promise

Great is his faithfulness; his mercies begin afresh each day.
LAMENTATIONS 3:23

Where He Leads Me

Written by Twila Paris
Recorded by Twila Paris
From the 1996 Dove Special Events Album of the Year

There's a great broad road through the meadow
And many travel there
But I have a gentle Shepherd
I would follow anywhere
Up a narrow path through the mountains
To the valley far below
To be ever in His presence
Where He leads me I will go

And there are many wondrous voices
Day and night they fill the air
There is one so small and quiet
I would know it anywhere
In the city or in the wilderness
There's a ringing crystal clear
And to be ever close beside Him
When He calls me I will hear

CHORUS
When He calls me I will hear
Where He leads me I will follow
When He calls me I will hear
Where He leads me I will follow
Where He calls me I will hear

There is a great broad road to nowhere
And so many travel there
But I have a gentle Shepherd
I would follow anywhere
Though the journey takes me far away
From the place I call my home

To be ever in His presence
Where He leads me I will go
Where He leads me I will go
Where He leads me I will go

WHERE HE LEADS ME

Stay the Course

In the wonderful movie *The African Queen,* Charlie Allnutt
(Humphrey Bogart) an unrefined, small-time African
riverboat operator and Rose Sayer (Katharine Hepburn),
a prim and proper British missionary are trying to navigate
Allnutt's boat, the *African Queen,* down a treacherous river
toward open waters. They endure being fired upon by
soldiers, jostled by tumultuous rapids, and munched upon
by swarms of insects. Suddenly, when it seems as if against
all odds they might make it to their destination, the river
spreads out and becomes shallow and choked with reeds.
Allnutt gets out of the boat and tries to pull it along, but
conditions only worsen until they're completely surrounded
and entangled, unable to move and unable to see where
they're going. With no way out and no food or water, they
give up and lie down to die.

Then in one of the most memorable shots in all of film history,
the camera pulls back to reveal that they're only a few yards
away from their goal! Because of the obstacles right in front of
their faces, they can't see the open lake—they can't see that the
big picture is good! During the night it rains, and when they
awaken they're floating free in the lake, their prayers answered.

Have you ever felt like God was leading you to a dead end?

237

Following the path God leads you on can be very unsettling at times. Often it's a difficult one. Your path may not have soldiers, rapids, and insects, but whatever trials and roadblocks you encounter may sometimes test your faith beyond what you think you can handle. But God never leads you down any road to abandon you. He may not act in your time frame or in quite the way you expected, but you can be sure he's there. In fact, it's at that very point where you feel that you've reached the end of yourself—at your wits' end and out of solutions—that you'll find the God who is strongest in your weakness, requiring only your trust in him (see 2 Corinthians 12:9).

Along the way there may be times you are tempted to give up. Others who've taken the path of least resistance will call out to you. "Hey, over here! This is the easy way!" Well meaning though they may be, you must seek God's will and choose the path you feel he has for your life. "The Lord says, 'I will guide you along the best pathway for your life. I will advise you and watch over you'" (Psalm 32:8). Far too often the easy way leads in the direction of sin and death.

My father has always said, "Do the hard thing first." It took me some time to grasp how profound and broadly applicable that statement really is. Think about it. If you want to enjoy good health, *first* you must exercise and watch your diet (hard). If you want good job opportunities, *first* you must work diligently on your education (hard). If you want to become accomplished as an athlete or musician or painter, *first* you must practice hours a day for several years (hard).

If you want your children to grow up to be confident, productive citizens, *first* you have to invest in their lives with love and discipline (hard). And, hardest of all, if you want to serve others and live for Christ, *first* you have to turn away from serving yourself and choose the path least traveled.

It was poet Robert Frost who said, "Two roads diverged in

a wood, and I—I took the one less traveled by, And that has made all the difference."

Money, fame, power—those are the roads on which most of us want to travel. We follow the bright lights of this culture only to discover that like holograms, they look like the real thing from a distance, but up close they're transparent and their promises are empty.

We have to be still and listen for God's voice. We live in a noisy world, and the devil has a megaphone. The huckster who shouts loudest does so because he has nothing worth buying. It's the still small voice that has what we need. We won't find it down just any old path. It's the narrow, less traveled one. You have to search for it.

So don't be discouraged if the path seems hard right now. Stay the course. As the apostle Paul said, "I am . . . forgetting the past and looking forward to what lies ahead" (Philippians 3:13). You're going for the best that God has to offer. And if all you can see is a river choked with reeds, you may be closer to the goal than you think.

A Closer Connection
When the path you are on is difficult, where do you turn for directions? Pray for discernment as you make choices about the road you will take.

A Challenge and . . .
The highway to hell is broad, and its gate is wide for the many who choose the easy way. But the gateway to life is small, and the road is narrow, and only a few ever find it. MATTHEW 7:13-14

A Promise
I have come as a light to shine in this dark world, so that all who put their trust in me will no longer remain in the darkness. JOHN 12:46

239

Wonderful, Merciful Savior

Written by Dawn Rodgers and Eric Wyse
Recorded by Selah
2002 Dove Nominee for Inspirational Recorded Song of the Year

Wonderful merciful Savior
Precious Redeemer and Friend
Who would have thought that a Lamb could
Rescue the souls of men
Oh You rescue the souls of men

Counselor Comforter Keeper
Spirit we long to embrace
You offer hope when our hearts have
Hopelessly lost the way
Oh we hopelessly lost the way

CHORUS
You are the One that we praise
You are the One we adore
You give the healing and grace
Our hearts always hunger for
Oh our hearts always hunger for

Almighty infinite Father
Faithfully loving Your own
Here in our weakness You find us
Falling before Your throne
Oh we're falling before Your throne

WONDERFUL,
MERCIFUL SAVIOR
The Face of Compassion

As Christians sometimes we tend to think of mercy in biblical terms, as if it's something only Christ can extend. But there are startling acts of mercy in our contemporary culture if we but look for them. Illinois governor George Ryan's decision on January 11, 2003, to commute all 156 of the state's death-row inmates' sentences to life in prison is a perfect example. While one might argue with the politics of such a decision, there's no doubt about its merciful nature.

Merriam Webster's Collegiate Dictionary defines *mercy* as "compassion shown to an offender; also, imprisonment rather than death imposed as penalty for first-degree murder." Ryan's act certainly measures up to both of these definitions.

History also has its share of merciful acts. For example, through her reforms of hospital sanitation during the Crimean War, Florence Nightingale put an end to the unnecessary deaths of wounded soldiers. This would qualify as mercy under another of *Webster's* definitions of *mercy:* "compassionate treatment of those in distress."

It has been said that grace is getting what you don't deserve and mercy is *not* getting what you do deserve. That brings us to one more of *Webster's* definitions of *mercy:* "a blessing that is an act of divine favor or compassion."

All of us, with some thought, could come up with many of our own stories of how Christ has shown us mercy in our lives. Offering hope when we have felt hopeless, forgiveness when we felt unforgivable, and healing when we were broken. But then that has always been the heart of Christ. Just look at the New Testament.

The Gospels of Matthew, Mark, and Luke all share the

accounts of Jesus healing a man with leprosy, healing a paralytic man, healing Peter's mother-in-law, raising a widow's son from the dead, healing a bleeding woman, restoring a girl to life, healing a demon-possessed boy, and healing a blind beggar.

Matthew 9:36 says, "He felt great pity for the crowds that came, because their problems were so great and they didn't know where to go for help. They were like sheep without a shepherd." Showing compassion, he then asks the disciples to pray for more workers for the harvest fields. In Mark 8:2-3 Jesus again shows compassion: "I feel sorry for these people. They have been here with me for three days, and they have nothing left to eat. And if I send them home without feeding them, they will faint along the road. For some of them have come a long distance."

In John 8 Jesus forgives an adulterous woman. In Matthew 15 and Mark 7 Jesus heals many people, and in Matthew 14 and Mark 6 he heals all who touch him. In Luke 7 he raises a widow's son from the dead!

Everything about Christ's ministry resonated with mercy. Again and again he put the concerns and feelings of others above himself. Then finally, in the greatest and most merciful act of all human history, Jesus went to the cross, taking all of our mistakes upon himself and making eternal freedom available to us all.

With such an example of mercy as our Lord, how can we not hunger for a closer relationship with him? If we love him, how can we not strive to be there for one another as he has been there for us?

The Lord we serve is the very face of compassion. Let us proclaim him to the world in the words of our mouths and the works of our hands so that all will know that he is a wonderful merciful Savior.

A Closer Connection

How many different ways have you been shown mercy by our Lord? Look for ways to extend mercy to others in the course of your daily life.

A Challenge and . . .

You must be compassionate, just as your Father is compassionate. LUKE 6:36

A Promise

God blesses those who are merciful, for they will be shown mercy. MATTHEW 5:7 *Lord help me to show mercy to others.*

You'll Be There

Written by Cindy Morgan
Recorded by Cindy Morgan
From the 1996 Dove Special Events Album of the Year

You were there when the lightning fell
Crashing down in the blue night
You came in like a raging wind all around
What a sweet light
And in the darkness You were there
And in the good times You were there
So let me say

With a prayer
Sweetest Savior who cares
Angels dance in the air
And tell us You'll be there

In the days when the dark and haze gather 'round
You're the rescue
You breathe again and the sun shines in
Through the clouds
How we need You
To be near and to be sovereign
Giving hope to each tomorrow
So we say

With a prayer
Sweetest Savior who cares
Angels dance in the air
And tell us You'll be there

Shadow the lightning
When we are frightened
Heavenly light keep shining on me
Shining on me

Everywhere
Sweetest Savior who cares
Angels dance in the air
And tell us
You'll be there

YOU'LL BE THERE

Hope on Both Sides of Heaven

After the tragedy on September 11, 2001, many people asked
the same question that is always heard in the wake of a
horrific event. Where was God?

I've never understood why people are so slow to credit
God for the blessings and gifts of their day-to-day lives but
so quick to blame God when something goes terribly wrong.
Maybe it's just our need for understanding. If it's all God's
fault when something goes wrong, then at least we know
where the problem is, and it's not us.

All right, you say. Fine. But what about the question?
Where was God on September 11?

God was in the heroism and selflessness of the rescue
workers, who continually risked their lives going back into
the burning towers time after time to help those trapped
inside; in the two men who carried a wheelchair-bound
woman down seventy flights of stairs to safety; in the people
who stood in line to give blood, even as they themselves
were bleeding; and in all the acts of courage and assistance
given inside the towers that we will never know about
because of those who didn't make it out. God was in the
people. God was in the love and comfort given by the victims

to one another. Even in unspeakable moments of terror and death, God was in the towers and on the planes and at the Pentagon. And as the world came together to mourn, God was in the prayers and outpouring of goodwill that came from every corner of the globe.

It is in community with one another that we most clearly see the hand of God in this world. It is in our acts of service to one another. It is caring more about others than we do about ourselves. For several weeks after 9/11 all of us did just that. But *whenever* we feed the hungry, take care of the sick, visit the imprisoned, extend justice to the oppressed—in short, whenever we love our neighbor, God is present.

But God is not only there when we're sad. He is also there when we rejoice together. Marriages, births, graduations, and anniversaries—whenever we gather to celebrate our love together—God is there.

Throughout every minute of our lives he is as close as the nearest prayer. It seems there could be no more comforting or amazing thought. But, as Christians, we believe there is a promise of something even more incredible—an eternal life in heaven through Jesus Christ, God's Son.

The Father cares enough to be with us when times are at their worst. He cares enough to be present with us when times are at their best. God laughs with us and cries with us. God gave us each other so that he can love us by caring for us and loving us through one another. Then in a final act of generous love and mercy, God sent his Son, Jesus, to us so that we could be set free of our sin and be united with him for eternity. Christ is our hope forever. He is the rescue. He is there for us not only in this present day but also for all the days to come, both here on earth and in heaven.

Tragedies will come. Life on earth will cause pain. To think otherwise is to ignore the way of things. But we needn't face the trials this world has to offer or fear what lies beyond the grave alone. The love of God through Christ Jesus stands ready to meet us on both sides of heaven. He'll be there.

A Closer Connection

How are you helping to make Christ's presence manifest in this world? If someone told you God had abandoned him or her, what would you say? Pray for an awareness of Christ's presence in all times and places, good or bad.

A Challenge . . .

Trust in the Lord always, for the Lord God is the eternal Rock.
ISAIAH 26:4

A Promise

God has put all things under the authority of Christ, and he gave him this authority for the benefit of the church. And the church is his body; it is filled by Christ, who fills everything everywhere with his presence.   EPHESIANS 1:22-23

Appendix A:

Above All
© 1995 Integrity Hosanna! Music / Lensongs Publishing, Inc.

Adonai
© 1997 Definitive Music (Admin. by Dayspring Music, Inc.), Dayspring Music, Inc. /Sparrow Song, Birdwing Music (All rights administered by EMI Christian Music Publishing.)

Another Time, Another Place
© 1990 Word Music, Inc., Housewife Music

Awesome God
© 1988 BMG Songs, Inc. ASCAP

Be the One
© 1990 First Verse Music/ John T. Benson Pub. Co. Inc. / Paragon Music ASCAP (Administered by Brentwood-Benson Music Publishing, Inc.) All rights reserved. Used by permission.

Because He Lives
© 1971 Gaither Music Co.

Blessed
© 2000 BMG Music, Inc. / Word Music Inc., Lola Max Music (Administered by Word Music, Inc.)

Circle of Friends
© 1996 Lehsem Music, LLC ASCAP Administered by Music & Media, Intl. /River Oaks Music Company BMI (All rights administered by EMI Christian Music Publishing.)

Dive
© 1999 Sparrow Song / Peach Hill Songs BMI (All rights administered by EMI Christian Music Publishing.)

El Shaddai
© 1993 Mole End Music (Administered by Word Music, Inc.)

Embrace the Cross
© 1989 BMG Songs, Inc. / Pamela Kay Music ASCAP (All rights administered by EMI Christian Music Publishing.)

Every Season
© 2000 Ariose Music Group, Inc. ASCAP (All rights administered by EMI Christian Music Publishing.)

Farther Than Your Grace Can Reach
© 1996 Lehsem Music LLC ASCAP Administered by Music & Media, Intl.

For All the World
© 1990 Lehsem Music, Inc. LLC ASCAP Administered by Music & Media, Intl. / Dayspring Music Inc., Summerdawn Music

For Future Generations
© 1994 Word Music, Inc. / A-Knack-For-This-Music / Paragon Music Co. Ltd./ New Spring Publishing, Inc. / Point Clear Music ASCAP (Administered by Brentwood-Benson Music Publishing, Inc.) All rights reserved. Used by permission.

For the Sake of the Call
© 1990 Careers-BMG Music Publishing, Inc. / Sparrow Song, Greg Nelson Music BMI (All rights administered by EMI Christian Music Publishing.)

Forever
© 2001 worshiptogether.com songs / Six Steps Music / ASCAP (All rights administered by EMI Christian Music Publishing.)

Friend of a Wounded Heart
© 1987 Word Music, Inc. ASCAP

God Is in Control
© 1993 Ariose Music Group, Inc., Mountain Spring Music ASCAP (All rights administered by EMI Christian Music Publishing.)

God of Wonders
© 2000 New Spring Publishing, Inc. / Never Say Never Songs / ASCAP (Administered by Brentwood-Benson Music Publishing, Inc.) All rights reserved. Used by permission. / Meaux Mercy / Strom Boy Music BMI (All rights administered by EMI Christian Music Publishing.)

God Will Make a Way
© 1990 Integrity Hosanna! Music

The Great Adventure
© 1992 Sparrow Song, Peach Hill Songs BMI Songs on the Forefront SESAC (All rights administered by EMI Christian Music Publishing.)

The Great Divide
© 1996 River Oaks Music Company BMI (Administered by EMI Christian Music Publishing.) / Emily Boothe (Administered by BMG Music Publishing, Inc.)

He Is
© 1994 Birdwing Music ASCAP Shepherd's Fold Music BMI (All rights administered by EMI Christian Music Publishing.)

He Is Exalted
© 1995 Straightway Music, Inc. / Mountain Spring Music ASCAP (All rights administered by EMI Christian Music Publishing.)

He Walked a Mile
© 1997 Songs of Lehsem SESAC Administered by Music & Media, Intl.

A Heart like Mine
© 1995 Word Music, Inc., Fanatic Music (Admin. by Word Music, Inc.), Dayspring Music, Inc., Summerdawn Music, Bob Farrell Music, Nanacub Music

The Heart of Worship
© 1999 Thankyou Music/PRS. Administered worldwide by worshiptogether.com Songs except for the UK and Europe which is administered by Kingsway Music.

His Strength Is Perfect
© 1998 Sparrow Song/ Greg Nelson Music ASCAP (All rights administered by EMI Christian Music Publishing.) / Multisongs (A Division of Careers-BMG Music Publishing, Inc.) SESAC Careers-BMG Music Publishing, Inc.

Home Free
© 1990 Material Music (Administered by Word Music, Inc.) / Word Music, Inc. ASCAP

How Beautiful
© 1991 Ariose Music / Mountain Spring Music ASCAP (All rights administered by EMI Christian Music Publishing.)

I Belong to Jesus!
© 1994 Shepherd's Heart Music, Inc. (Admin. by Dayspring Music, Inc.)

I Pledge Allegiance to the Lamb
© 1994 Shepherd Boy (Administered by Word Music, Inc.) / Word Music, Inc.

I Surrender All
©1994 First Verse Music ASCAP (Administered by Brentwood-Benson Music Publishing, Inc.) All rights reserved. Used by permission. / Songs of Lehsem SESAC Administered by Music & Media, Intl.

I've Just Seen Jesus
©1985 Gaither Music Co. ASCAP / Ariose Music (All rights administered by EMI Christian Music Publishing.)

I Will Follow Christ

In Christ Alone

Jesus Freak

Jesus King of Angels

Jesus Will Still Be There

King of Glory

Lord of the Dance

A Man after Your Own Heart

More Than Wonderful

On My Knees

Place in This World

Redeemer

Rise Again
© 1977 Going Home Music SESAC / Dimension Music (SESAC) / Administered by Integrated Copyright Group

Say the Name
© 1993 His Eye Music, Maggie Bees Music SESAC Sparrow Song BMI (All rights administered by EMI Christian Music Publishing.)

Shine
© 1994 Ariose Music ASCAP (All rights administered by EMI Christian Music Publishing) / Warner Sojourner Music / Soylent Tunes Administered by Integrated Copyright Group

Shout to the Lord
© 1997 Integrity Hosanna! Music

Sometimes He Calms the Storm
© 1995 BMG Songs, Inc. ASCAP / Careers-BMG Music Publishing, Inc., BMI

Sometimes Miracles Hide
© 1991 Word Music, Inc. ASCAP / Lehsem Music LLC ASCAP Administered by Music & Media, Intl.

Step by Step
© 1991 BMG Songs, Inc. (ASCAP) and Kid Brothers of St. Frank Publishing. All rights on behalf of Kid Brothers of St. Frank Publishing administered by BMG Songs, Inc.

Thank You
© 1988 Ray Boltz /Administered by Gaither Music Company

Watercolour Ponies
© 1987 Word Music, Inc.

We Fall Down
© 1997 BMG Songs, Inc. / Above The Rim Music ASCAP

Where He Leads Me
© 1995 Ariose Music / Mountain Spring Music ASCAP (All rights administered by EMI Christian Music Publishing.)

Wonderful, Merciful Savior
© 1989 Word Music Inc., Dayspring Music, Inc.

You'll Be There
© 1996 Word Music, Inc.

Notes

Blessed

Quote by Charles Swindoll, "Attitudes," can be found at <www.businesspipeline.com/pressreleases/poem_3htm> .

Embrace the Cross

Oswald Chambers, *My Utmost for His Highest,* ed. James Reimann (Grand Rapids, Mich.: Discovery House, 1992), 9/1, 6/14.

Dietrich Bonhoeffer, *The Cost of Discipleship* (New York: Touchstone, 1995), 43.

For Future Generations

Steve Farrar, *Anchor Man: How a Father Can Anchor His Family in Christ for the Next 100 Years* (Nashville: Nelson, 1998), 7–8.

For the Sake of the Call

Charles Sheldon, *In His Steps,* ed. James S. Bell Jr. (Tulsa, Okla.: Honor Books, 1998).

Forever

Quote by Branch Rickey can be found at www.baseball-almanac.com/quotes/quobr.shtml.

Friend of a Wounded Heart

Dale T. Irvin and Scott W. Sunquist, *History of the World Christian Movement* (Maryknoll, N.Y.: Orbis, 2001), 155.

Charles Colson, "Identifying with Jesus" in *NIV Men's Devotional Bible: New International Version* (Grand Rapids, Mich.: Zondervan, 1993), 1021.

The Great Adventure

Annie Dillard, *Teaching a Stone to Talk* (New York: Harper, 1982), 58–59.

Dr. Dan Moseley quote is from a Sunday school class in 1993 at Vine Street Christian Church, Nashville, Tennessee.

He Is Exalted

Laurence Bergreen, *As Thousands Cheer: The Life of Irving Berlin* (New York: Da Capo Press, 1996).

C. S. Lewis quote.

How Beautiful

Mary Bray Pipher, *Reviving Ophelia: Saving the Selves of Adolescent Girls* (New York: Ballantine, 1994), 56.

I Pledge Allegiance to the Lamb

Jock Purves, *Fair Sunshine: Character Studies of the Scottish Covenanters* (London: Banner of Truth Trust, 1968), 80–82.

In Christ Alone

"It's Hard to Be Humble," words and music by Mac Davis. ©1979 Songpainter Music BMI.

Jesus Will Still Be There

Dr. Seuss, *Oh, the Places You'll Go* (New York: Random House, 1990).

On My Knees

Quotes from Dr. Lawrence Keene are from sermons delivered between October 1983 and April 1992 at the Little Brown Church of the Valley, North Hollywood, California, and the Church of the Valley, Van Nuys, California.

Place in This World

B. Kliban, *Whack Your Porcupine, and Other Drawings* (New York: Workman, 1977).

Rise Again

Quotes from "Medical Aspects of the Crucifixion of Jesus Christ," compiled by David Terasaka, M.D. ©1996. All rights reserved. http://www.new-life.net/crucify1.htm.

Shine

Walter Wangerin Jr., *Paul: a Novel* (Grand Rapids, Mich.: Zondervan, 2000), 170, 115.

Sometimes He Calms the Storm

Joe South, "I Never Promised You a Rose Garden," © 1977 Sony/ATV Music LLC.

Watercolour Ponies

For more on teaching children about God, see Focus on the Family's *Parents Guide to the Spiritual Growth of Children*, published by Tyndale House Publishers, 2000.

Where He Leads Me

Robert Frost, "The Road Not Taken" in *Robert Frost: Selected Poems* (New York: Gramercy Books, 2001).

Wonderful, Merciful Savior

Merriam Webster's Collegiate Dictionary, 10th ed., s.v. "mercy."

Topical Index

About the Author

Steve Siler has had over four hundred of his contemporary Christian songs recorded. Point of Grace, Avalon, Anointed, Clay Crosse, The Martins, Aaron Jeoffrey, Greg Long, BeBe Winans, Bob Carlisle, Scott Krippayne, and Tammy Trent are among the artists that have recorded his songs.

Siler has been nominated for four Dove Awards, winning the award for Inspirational Song of the Year in 2000 with "I Will Follow Christ." "Circle of Friends, " "Not Too Far from Here, " and "Farther Than Your Grace Can Reach" are his other best-known songs. In all, he has had nine number-one CCM songs and thirty-four top-ten singles.

Steve is the director of a nonprofit organization called Music for the Soul (www.musicforthesoul.org) that offers Christian-lyric content music to people dealing with issues of recovery.

He lives in Nashville, Tennessee, with his wife of twenty years, Meredith, and their two children.

GMA
GOSPEL MUSIC ASSOCIATION

A portion of the royalties from this book are being donated to the Gospel Music Association (a non-profit trade organization). The mission of the Gospel Music Association (GMA) is to expose, promote, and celebrate the gospel through music. The Dove Awards are determined each year by the voting membership of the GMA. To join GMA, visit **WWW.GOSPELMUSIC.ORG** for more information, or call (615) 242-0303. For information about the Dove Awards, including past winners, award categories, and important news announcements, please visit **WWW.DOVEAWARDS.COM**.

GMA 35TH
DOVE AWARDS